16:8

Intermittent Fasting

Jaime Rose Chambers is an accredited practising dietitian and nutritionist. She has a Bachelor of Nutrition & Dietetics from the University of Newcastle and is completing a Masters of Clinical Science for complementary therapies. She sees patients with a wide range of health conditions, including diabetes, obesity, food allergies and intolerances, polycystic ovarian syndrome and cancer. Jaime is a well-respected voice in diet and nutrition, and has made appearances on *Today Tonight* and *A Current Affair,* as well as being a frequent contributor to publications such as *The Australian Women's Weekly.* She also speaks regularly on the importance of nutrition at corporate seminars and cancer support groups.

16:8

Intermittent
Fasting

JAIME ROSE CHAMBERS

Pan Macmillan Australia

contents

PART TWO: RECIPES

Introduction

As a dietitian, I've been helping people lose weight and improve their health for a decade. There's no question that weight loss makes most people feel better – it can also save lives. This has been the basis of my work through my entire career. It's widely known that being overweight increases your risk of developing major chronic diseases such as heart disease, type 2 diabetes and certain cancers, as well as osteoarthritis. I've seen and heard about nearly every diet, fad and procedure for improving weight and health, and I've prescribed thousands of personalised meal plans over the years. But without a doubt, intermittent fasting is one of the most powerful tools for health and weight management I've seen, both in my personal and my professional life.

Until recently, we dietitians only had so many weight-loss strategies in our toolkit; we could recommend that our patients reduce their calories, count macronutrients, increase physical activity, cut out alcohol, lower carbohydrates and increase their protein intake. And of course beyond that, patients also had a wealth of fad diets to choose from – each claiming to be the answer to every weight-loss or health issue. And while it's true most diets work to a certain degree in the short term, some delivering quick and dramatic results, progress inevitably plateaus.

As it turns out, the hardest thing about losing weight is keeping it off! Dieters get sick of restricting food, gain weight over the holidays, have too many boozy weekends or stop exercising for a period due to injury. Or, they simply lose their motivation and revert back to old habits. In addition to these common pitfalls, there are also metabolic changes to contend with. When we follow a low-calorie diet long term, lean muscle can be reduced, causing our metabolism (i.e. the rate at which we burn energy) to slow down. Consequently, all of our hard work is quickly undone and we regain the lost weight, thus perpetuating the diet cycle

even further. Research shows that a mere one in six overweight and obese adults report maintaining a weight loss of at least 10 per cent for one year, at any point in their lives.

Weight-loss strategies divide the dietetic world. Is it better to support people to lose weight knowing they're likely to be unsuccessful maintaining that weight loss long term? Or, should we throw our hands up, agree that weight loss doesn't work and simply encourage patients to be okay with any extra weight they may be carrying? There's no doubt that the deck seems stacked against patients who want to lose weight and keep it off.

Enter fasting, the practice of going a set amount of time with little-to-no food. Fasting has been an integral part of many religions and cultures for centuries. It made its first scientific appearance in the 1930s, when researchers restricted the calories of rats. Not only did fasting not cause the rats to become malnourished, it appeared to prolong their lifespan, reduce their rates of cancer, diabetes and heart disease and improve certain inflammatory markers.

Intermittent fasting, which involves alternating periods of eating with short periods of fasting, has been on my radar since 2012. That year, I, along with millions of others, watched an episode of BBC TWO's *Horizon* called 'Eat, Fast and Live Longer'. Presented by Dr Michael Mosley, it covered the many health and weight-loss benefits of intermittent fasting. The evidence presented in that documentary sent the diet and nutrition world into a frenzy, and while I have a keen interest in anything new and shiny in the health sphere, the research was just too new for me to feel comfortable including intermittent fasting in my own practice – I needed more evidence. I was also concerned fasting would turn out to be yet another fad diet. Severely limiting calories for two days of the week also sounded hard going, and I thought it would be too difficult for most people to sustain.

About five years after watching that program I read a summary of the latest research on intermittent fasting from the University of Illinois at Chicago and was blown away! Not only were the metabolic and weight-loss benefits impressive, but there were also significant improvements in terms of long-term health outcomes. Now I had the research to back up this approach, and it was very compelling.

Up until this point, my dietary advice had been targeted to the particular outcome the patient was working towards. For example, I'd recommend that someone trying to lower their risk of heart disease avoid saturated and trans fats and eat more fibre-rich foods.

Without a doubt, intermittent fasting is one of the most powerful tools for health and weight management I've seen.

This is still relevant advice today, but now I also know that intermittent fasting helps reduce the risk of most major chronic diseases, and even demonstrates long-term disease prevention, with the added benefit of being a single (and simple) strategy to follow. So I use a variety of intermittent fasting regimes with many of my patients, and it has proved to be one of the most effective and easiest tools for successful and sustained weight and health management.

Although it's still early days in the world of intermittent fasting, I've never encountered a more potent or user-friendly way of manipulating weight and short-term health outcomes. The thing I love about intermittent fasting is that it's not a 'diet'. I once heard it referred to as a 'health strategy' and I think that describes it perfectly. When you're in fasting mode, it's only for a short time and it's over before you know it. When you're in eating mode, you're able to enjoy nourishing food as you normally would – there's no cutting out food groups (unless you need to for health reasons). As someone who loves food and whose entire career revolves around it, this makes my heart sing! Intermittent fasting really has revolutionised the way I do my job and how effectively I've been able to help my patients reach their goals.

The practice of intermittent fasting has evolved to embrace two main styles: part-day and full-day fasting. I'll cover both of these styles later on, and explain the varying forms and degrees of intensity within each style. I'll also share my own experiences of intermittent fasting, as well as several real-life case studies from my practice. Not only will you find a fasting regime that suits your health goals, you'll also be able to tailor it to your lifestyle and even tweak it as you go, depending on what your schedule looks like.

To many people, fasting sounds a little daunting. Often the first thing I hear when I bring up fasting with a patient is, 'So I can't eat anything all day?' But that's not the case. In fact, you can eat every day when you're fasting, no matter which form you choose. And the benefits beyond weight loss speak for themselves: I've observed my patients successfully reduce their total and 'bad' LDL cholesterol, reduce their blood pressure, blood sugar and insulin levels, report dramatically improved digestion – and even save money (up to $100 a week!).

So read on, and I'll walk you through the various fasting styles and their incredible health benefits, and show you what a structured, yet flexible, fasting journey looks like. I'll also share 40 wholesome recipes that I regularly make to ensure you enjoy your eating windows to the fullest. Each recipe is suited to a regular as well as a part-day fasting day, and they each feature a 5:2 modification, which means they can be easily adjusted if you're on a full-day fast. I really hope the information and recipes in this book help to make fasting one of the most powerful tools in your life, whatever your health, weight and lifestyle goals.

Jaime Chambers

 Although fasting benefits many people, it's not for everyone. There are individuals who should either seek medical support or advice before fasting, or who should avoid fasting altogether (see page 52 for more detail). This might be due to an unhealthy history with food or because of a vulnerable medical history that requires specialised advice and support.

PART ONE

why
fast?

Intermittent fasting has evolved to embrace two main styles: part- and full-day fasting.

My fasting story

Several years ago (before I started experimenting with intermittent fasting), my dad and stepmum started a 5:2 fast. Both were in great health, but each of them had medical and family histories that they thought might cause issues for them later in life. My dad's father had been diagnosed with early-onset Alzheimer's in his 60s and sadly lived in a vegetative state for many years before passing away. My stepmum was diagnosed with bowel cancer at 38 and had undergone a bowel resection and chemotherapy before meeting my dad. Though fertility had been a major concern for her, she managed to conceive my little brother (now 11) and has been all-clear for cancer ever since.

Dad has always been curious about anything to do with science and medicine, and he was intrigued by research indicating that intermittent fasting showed a lot of promise for protecting the brain against Alzheimer's and possibly slowing cancer tumour growth in animals. A bonus was that in the short term, both of them lost around 8 kilograms each following the 5:2 fast. They still fast for one to two days a week even now, depending on their schedules and health and weight goals. The long-term health effects, however, will not be known for many years to come.

TAKING THE LEAP

Although I followed my dad and stepmum's 5:2 journey with interest, it wasn't until I came across some particularly compelling research that intermittent fasting became the ultimate game-changer for me, and my career. The outcomes from the human and animal studies summarised in that research were quite incredible. But what was equally as exciting was discovering the range of fasting methods that are available, which is what makes this approach really flexible. From a practical perspective, this was wonderful for me because it meant I could tailor fasting regimes to my patients' individual needs rather than prescribe them one strict and unforgiving regime to follow.

I often try out dietary strategies before using them in my clinic so I fully understand what I'm asking my patients to do, and can relate to what they're going through if they've been following a particular diet. So what better way to really understand intermittent fasting than to give it a shot myself? I've never found it 'easy' to maintain my weight; I sit at the top end of the normal range,

It wasn't until I came across some particularly compelling research that intermittent fasting became the ultimate game-changer for me.

The regime that works best for me is a combination of the two fasting methods: full-day and part-day.

I eat well and exercise regularly, but I have a history of polycystic ovarian syndrome and an underactive thyroid, which I take medication for, and both of these conditions can make weight management a little tricky.

As usual, my husband was willing to be a human guinea pig with me. At the time I had recently had a baby and was about 3 kilograms above my normal weight, but about 5 kilograms heavier than I ultimately wanted to be as a healthy clinical goal. My husband also wanted to lose 5 kilograms, and he also had slightly elevated cholesterol and a strong family history of neurodegenerative disease. So our short-term goal was weight loss and our long-term goals were based on protecting our brains and reducing our overall risk of chronic disease.

On January 1st, we started our annual month of healthy eating and a regular exercise regime to reboot and reset healthy habits after the holiday season, and we made fasting a part of this. We started with the 5:2 method of fasting – 500 calories (2,090 kj) a day for me and 600 calories (2,508 kj) for my husband on two days of the week, and eating normally on the other five days of the week. We agreed we'd trial it for a month to see what happened.

The first week was pretty rough! We were both 'hangry' and fantasised about cheating in those difficult afternoon and after-dinner slots. But as we persevered it really did get easier and easier – to the point where we even looked forward to our fasting days. Although they were challenging, we felt pretty fantastic. We both found we felt lighter, more alert and energetic. Our digestion improved, our appetite dampened and we had fewer cravings for sweet foods. Six weeks into our fast we had both lost 3–4 kilograms and felt great. My husband's cholesterol had also come down.

LIFE HAPPENS!

After those first few challenging weeks, we finally hit our stride with fasting. We were doing so well and feeling great, but then our son started daycare and within a week the endless cycle of sickness began as he came down with every bug making its way around his classmates. The LAST thing I felt like doing when I was sleep deprived and mopping up vomit was fasting.

As time went on, I also found that I needed to be in tip-top shape in order to get through a full day of fasting. If I had a dinner on or a work function, I just wasn't interested. I would work my social events around those fasting days so nothing would tempt me. My husband noticed that his work was sometimes impacted on fasting days due to meetings, coffees and lunches with clients. As a long-term strategy, it became clear that 5:2 fasting was something we could do and get great results with, but only in fits and starts, with breaks in between.

Once our family was back to full health again, I was ready to get back into our fasting regime. This time though, we decided to trial part-day fasting, or 16:8 – where we would fast for 16 hours a day (mostly overnight while sleeping), and eat within an eight-hour window. We planned to do this three or more days a week, on workdays, with an 'eating window' from lunchtime until 8 pm (we like to eat dinner together).

Part-day fasting was certainly a much easier strategy to follow for us. I'm not usually very hungry in the mornings, and am happy to subsist on a good coffee until late morning. My husband, on the other hand, is a big breakfast eater and relies on it to get him moving through the day. As with the first few days of our 5:2 fast, initially this first week was a bit of a challenge – feeling my empty, grumbly tummy and trying to resist a lovely milky coffee – but then it got easier and easier. Overall, part-day fasting required much less effort and thought than full-day fasting because it didn't require calorie counting or meal-planning. And, once the fasting period was over, we could eat whatever we wanted as long as we ate during that eight-hour window.

HOW FASTING WORKS FOR US

My husband loves this form of part-day fasting – the biggest differences are that he feels energetic and clear-headed in the morning and his afternoon energy crashes have improved, though they are still determined by the food choices he makes at lunchtime. Now at his ideal weight, part-day fasting is part of his weekly routine. By eating within an eight-hour time frame three days a week, he easily maintains his weight.

I, on the other hand, found using part-day fasting as my only regime tricky. I love food – I'm constantly creating and testing recipes for my job, or working on my laptop from cafes where I love having eggs or a warm porridge in the morning. I'm also up at 5 am most days (courtesy of a tiny person), so waiting until midday to eat could be rough.

The regime that works best for me is a combination of the two fasting methods: full-day and part-day. I can easily manage one full-day fast a week. Tuesdays are a busy clinic day for me: I race out of the house, drop off my baby at his grandparents' then I'm back-to-back with patients all day, so sailing through the day on reduced calories is fine. Then, depending on what the rest of my week looks like, I slot in one or two part-day fasts. Thursdays often work well because I do a Mums & Bubs exercise class and by the time we get home it's time to break my fast with a yummy lunch. Saturdays are a busy clinic morning for me, so that works as a part-day fasting day too.

Through trial and error, and by monitoring my body's response to intermittent fasting, I've discovered that my current regime is enough to keep my weight stable. If at any point I want to get into weight-loss mode, perhaps after a holiday or a string of big social events, I know I can ramp things up a little. I may either do two full-day fasting days or I might continue with the one full fasting day and do four or five part-day fasting days. I might also increase my exercise a little, depending on what I've been doing and if I have the time and capacity for it.

As with any health strategy, fasting won't be for everyone (see page 52), but the flexibility of these regimes means that you can tailor and constantly manipulate how you fast. Not only does this mean you can get the results you want, it also means you can sustain them by making intermittent fasting part of your life forever so you can reap the long-term benefits later. This is medical music to my ears!

Do the sums

One of the less obvious benefits to fasting is to our back pockets! If you're skipping a meal and a morning snack most days, at the very least this is likely to save you about $25 on coffees each week and up to $100 if you're skipping bought breakfasts. If, on some days, you're only eating 500 or 600 calories (2,090 or 2,508 kj) and mostly bringing your food from home, that's the equivalent of around one-and-a-half day's worth of food that you don't need to account for. Bonus!

CASE STUDY
Jane: THE BUSY (MENOPAUSAL) MUM

Jane was 51 years old when she came to see me. Up until she had reached menopause, she'd easily maintained a normal, healthy weight of 55 kilograms. But when Jane hit menopause at 49, without making any changes to her diet or lifestyle she gained 7 kilograms over a 12–18 month period. Where once she'd been able to go on holiday, gain a couple of kilos and lose them easily once she returned home, she noticed that her weight was going up but she just couldn't get it to come back down again.

Jane had a history of a thyroid autoimmune condition called Hashimoto's, which can affect weight. However she was on medication for that and her most recent biochemistry showed her hormone levels to be normal.

Jane lives with her husband and two teenage sons and works long hours in a corporate job. She doesn't get home until 7.30 pm most nights, so her husband cooks dinner during the week. Jane has always had routine eating habits and is very disciplined when it comes to exercise, training six days a week. She also enjoys half a bottle of wine with her husband three nights a week.

Jane had tried increasing her already intense exercise and restricting her daily calories, particularly the carbohydrate portions, but found she was just so hungry and her weight didn't budge at all. Her experience is a very common one for women who reach menopause, particularly that weight gain around the abdomen due to the hormonal changes that occur. However there's no reason why normal weight can't be maintained through menopause; it just requires some smart and careful adjustments.

Jane already had so many positive health behaviours so I didn't want to disrupt her routine too much, but that also didn't leave me with much to work with to get her burning fat. This is where intermittent fasting can be brilliant because routines can generally stay the same. I recommended she try the 16:8 part-day fasting method seven days a week, so we were simply limiting her eating window to eight hours of the day. Because she was already eating her first meal of the day after she exercised on weekends, fasting wouldn't disrupt her weekend routine either.

After two weeks, Jane returned and was concerned she hadn't lost any weight. But after we took her measurements she was very happy to see she had lost 1.7 kilograms and 2–3 cm around her abdomen and hips. Two weeks later, she'd lost another 2 cm from her abdomen. And a fortnight later, she'd lost another 2 kilograms and 2 cm from around her abdomen. After five months of 16:8 fasting Jane has reached her weight goal and reports that she loves fasting in the mornings, and that this will be her routine for life now.

> **There's no reason why normal weight can't be maintained through menopause; it just requires some smart and careful adjustments.**

How IF is different

There are thousands of diets and weight-loss programs out there – from eating cabbage soup or eliminating grains, to drinking meal-replacement shakes or surgically removing part of the stomach. But after a period of dieting, our body adapts to the lower calories and weight loss ceases. We also experience something known as 'diet fatigue' (see page 54), which can happen at any time, and loss of motivation is usually to blame. This is part of the reason why most diets are unsuccessful.

The beauty of intermittent fasting is that it makes it harder for the body to adapt to long-term calorie restriction because you are still eating normally some of the time. And, because fasting doesn't require cutting out food groups, it's easier to satisfy your body's nutritional requirements. And psychologically, there are no restrictions when you're not fasting – all foods and eating occasions can be enjoyed!

Here are some of the many benefits of intermittent fasting:

- √ Unlike other diets, you don't need to fast every day, or even every hour of the day

- √ When you're not fasting you can eat with no restrictions

- √ It can be more sustainable in the long term than a traditional low-calorie diet

- √ It's flexible and can be tailored to your lifestyle

- √ It can help with weight loss, but the benefits go beyond weight loss

- √ It targets abdominal fat, which is associated with an increased risk of chronic disease

- √ It can help to reduce the risk of most major chronic diseases

- √ It can help reduce blood sugar levels, insulin, cholesterol, blood pressure and inflammation

- √ It can help protect the brain against degenerative diseases

- √ You don't have to omit any food groups

- √ It may help to reduce 'junk' food cravings

- √ It encourages getting in touch with your body's needs and hunger cues, and is not about deprivation

- √ Calorie-counting (for those following a full-day fasting regime) can increase knowledge and awareness of the energy value of food

- √ It encourages planning ahead

- √ Food is often more enjoyable.

Fasting methods explained

Intermittent fasting involves alternating fasting periods with times of eating. Avoiding food completely, or restricting it dramatically, is known as the 'fasting period'. The period of time for eating is known in the wider fasting and diet community as 'feasting', however in this book, I refer to it as the 'eating window'. This is because the word feasting is associated with overeating and implies extreme and contradictory behaviour – fasting vs. feasting. Although you can eat well and enjoy wholesome food with no rules or restrictions during the eating window, it isn't a free-for-all, but rather a time for what I prefer to think of as conscious nourishing.

Although there are many different methods of fasting (ranging from hours to days, and from no food to limited food), I concentrate on two methods only in this book because they are the most well-researched (and, I believe, the most easily adaptable and sustainable).

The first of these fasting methods is what I refer to as **PART-DAY FASTING** (also known as time-restricted feeding, 16:8 or 18:6). In this method, you fast completely (i.e. avoid all calories) for a set number of hours each day.

The second fasting method is **FULL-DAY FASTING** (also known as 5:2, 6:1 or alternate-day fasting), where you eat just a quarter of your daily calories over a full day, but only on certain days of the week.

Research has not yet been conducted on comparing part-day and full-day fasting methods, so we don't yet know which is the better method. What we do know is that any type of fasting can have positive health and weight-loss benefits, so the most important factor is finding the method that is right for you.

FASTING STYLE 1: *Part-day*

Part-day fasting, otherwise known as time-restricted feeding, 16:8 or 18:6, is generally the most user-friendly and sustainable method of intermittent fasting. Simply put, you fast for a certain number of hours (either 16 or 18) each day, and then follow your normal diet for the balance of the day (i.e. eight or six hours). This approach is very popular because there's no need to count calories, watch your portion sizes, feel deprived or restricted or miss out on social occasions. Of all the fasting methods, the compliance rate is highest on 16:8. This is the method people are most able to stick to in the long term.

Fasting for even just 12 hours of the day (i.e. not eating between 7 pm and 7 am) can be a challenge for some people. Most of us eat well into the night or in the early morning, whether we're getting home late from work and throwing together pasta at 9 pm, nibbling on chocolate or popcorn while we watch Netflix after dinner, or revving up with a milky coffee at 6 am. This means we're not eating for about eight or nine hours of the day. But in order to get into fat-burning mode, our body needs to fast for at least 12 hours.

Part-day fasting takes the philosophy of fasting for part of the day to the next level by encouraging fasting for more than 12 hours of the day. This allows the body to have a rest from constantly processing energy and fuel and gives us an opportunity to access and burn our fat stores for fuel to achieve weight loss.

One of the benefits of part-day fasting is that it encourages us to eat earlier in the evening. According to Dr Michael Mosley, our body is preparing for sleep from around 8 pm, so our blood sugar and fat levels begin to rise as our body prepares for the overnight fast. If we eat late into the evening, this drives up blood sugar and encourages it to stay higher for longer.

Almost anyone can benefit from this style of fasting. It's the most adaptable style because it is not extreme, is very flexible and is generally safe, as long as nutritional needs are met. But, as with any health strategy, there is a small group of people for whom fasting may not be suitable (see page 52).

In general, part-day fasting suits most people, including:

✓ Those who generally aren't very hungry at certain times of the day

✓ Busy mums and dads (it's one less meal/snack to make!)

✓ Shift workers

✓ Those who travel for work (limit eating to an eight-hour window on a flight and then when overseas, simply skip breakfast or dinner)

✓ People on holiday (whether on a beach break or a European adventure, sleep in and skip breakfast or enjoy the breakfast buffet and stop eating after a late lunch).

✓ People who can't do full-day fasting because their jobs

  - are very physically active (i.e. builders);
  - require complex thinking (i.e. lawyers); or
  - demand that they are in top physical shape (i.e. surgeons).

✓ Those who like to eat a proper family meal together in the morning or evening

✓ Anyone concerned or apprehensive about doing full-day fasting.

Although there are many different methods of fasting (ranging from hours to days, and from no food to limited food), I focus on two methods in this book because they are the most well-researched.

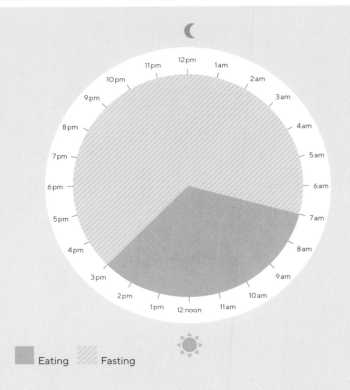

Eating   Fasting

16:8

The 16:8 fasting method means that you fast for 16 hours in a 24-hour period, and eat only within an eight-hour window. The good news is that most of your fasting hours will fall during the hours you are asleep, making it far more manageable. The eight-hour eating window can then be whenever suits you.

Although the 16:8 method is the simplest way to part-day fast, ultimately eating within just a 12-hour window can have positive health and weight benefits. Achieving change depends on your starting point. For example, if you eat breakfast at 7 am, finish dinner by 7 pm and don't snack after dinner, you are already eating within a 12-hour window. To experience improved health benefits, you'll need to narrow your eating window. This can be done incrementally, perhaps by pushing breakfast back by an hour or two for a few weeks and monitoring the results. Or you could start straight onto a 16:8 regime, where your eating window is reduced to eight hours a day.

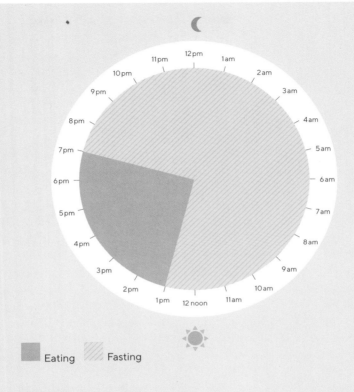

Eating   Fasting

18:6

This method of fasting is exactly the same as 16:8 except it is slightly more intense because you fast for 18 hours of the day and eat within a six-hour window. So, for example, you may fast until 1 pm, and then have your eating window until 7 pm, when you begin fasting again.

The same strategies apply for this form of part-day fasting, but I only suggest following this method if you are able to meet your nutritional requirements in the shortened timeframe.

When should I eat?

If you really enjoy breakfast or feel a bit wobbly if you don't start the day with something to eat, for 16:8 you may want to break your fast at 8 am, which means your eating window will close at 4 pm. If you're not terribly hungry first thing in the morning but get ravenous by mid-morning, you could break your fast at around 10 am, then begin fasting again at 6 pm.

By far, the most popular regime among my patients (and the one I prefer) is to fast until lunchtime – midday – then begin fasting again around 8 pm. This allows you to break your fast with a hearty lunch, have the option to snack during that difficult 3 pm dip, and then enjoy dinner with your family, or social time in the evenings. Ultimately, the hours that work best for you are very personal and may vary from day to day or week to week.

Keep in mind that if you're part-day fasting most days, the times of day you choose to eat need to stay fairly consistent, otherwise your fasting window the following day will be thrown out a little. Any fast for 12 hours or more can be beneficial, so if you do move your times around a little, you will still get the metabolic and health benefits, though you might just find managing your appetite for longer fasting periods trickier. If you want to adjust your eating window, my suggestion is to do it gradually by one to two hours each day. The other option is to have a non-fasting day in between the days you want to change your fasting schedule, then just start afresh, scheduling your eating window when best suits you.

What can I eat when I'm fasting?

That's easy: nothing! With part-day fasting, you must completely fast during the hours you aren't eating. That means no food or drinks that contain any calories. This is to prevent an increase in your blood glucose and insulin levels, which will bump you out of fasting mode.

Here's what you can have:

* Water
* Sparkling or still mineral water
* Herbal tea*
* Black coffee*
* Black tea*

* You can use sweeteners such as stevia, Splenda or Equal, if you must.
  But it is preferable to avoid sweeteners for your general health.

But what if I hate black coffee/tea?

The calorie-free teas and coffees can be the biggest barrier for some people on the 16:8 fasting regime, often because they hate black coffee or tea. If this is the case, it's better to add a 'dash' (½ to 1 tablespoon) of milk to your coffee than to not fast at all.

Another consideration here is using milks that contain little to no carbohydrates or sugars (whether natural sugars such as lactose in cow's milk or added sugars from milks such as oat or soy). Milks such as unsweetened almond and coconut milk are a better choice because they have almost no sugars, which is what will trigger the blood glucose and insulin response that may bump you out of fasting mode. However, if weight loss is a goal of yours, be mindful that coconut milk is generally very rich in calories due to the natural fats found in coconut.

What can I eat when I'm ... eating?

Here's some great news: during your eating window, you can enjoy what you normally eat – no restrictions! You don't need to cut out food groups, count calories, weigh or measure foods or skip tasty sauces or dressings. In a nutshell, you don't need to be in 'diet' mode.

Unlike a traditional calorie-controlled diet, you need to think more about foods you DO need to eat in order to meet your nutritional requirements, rather than what you should be avoiding. This is really important, particularly when you're limiting your eating day and potentially missing one or two meals or snacks where you'd normally get certain nutrients.

Here's a common scenario I see with morning fasters. Breakfast is a meal that often provides two of our dairy serves; these might be in the form of a latte and milk with a bowl of cereal. But if a person begins to fast in the morning and skips this meal, they may not meet their calcium requirements. So it's essential they find other ways to include that dairy in their eating window (see page 86 for meal plans).

How often should I fast?

How many days a week you choose to fast is really up to you. It depends on a number of factors such as how much sticking to this regime is going to impact your life, what your weekly schedule looks like and what your health and weight goals are. My recommendations are to fast anywhere from three to seven days a week.

Research shows that doing a part-day fast for as little as three days a week can be beneficial. It's important to keep in mind, though, that most research is conducted on people who already have a high starting weight, so they may be considered clinically overweight, which means they have a body mass index (BMI) of 25–30, or obese (a BMI of 30 or more). In those cases, even just a few small adjustments to eating can make quite a significant difference to weight and health outcomes.

If, however, your weight and health, as well as your general diet and activity, are closer to ideal or 'normal' and you just want to lose a few kilograms, then three days a week of fasting may not be enough for you to see any significant changes. On the other hand, if weight loss is not your goal and you simply want to prevent chronic disease over the long term, reduce your cholesterol, blood pressure, blood glucose or insulin levels and protect your brain as you age, three days a week of fasting might be perfect for you.

As with any lifestyle change, it's good to start small and build up. This is beneficial from a behavioural perspective because making incremental changes to your routine can be much easier to manage as it's not too different to what you're currently doing. The other reason is that this gives you room to move, and another stage or step you can progress to if your weight plateaus or certain health indicators (like cholesterol levels) level out.

For many of my patients who work regular Monday to Friday jobs, fasting on their five working days is an easy way to incorporate this regime into their week. Generally, meals and snacks are quite routine on workdays, so simply limiting the eating window often works a treat.

For patients who are shift workers, such as nurses, I find 16:8 fasting is the perfect method because they can simply shuffle their eating window around depending on their shifts. Even so, some shift workers prefer not to eat during their shift if it is overnight. Again, this comes down to personal preference, but the regime is flexible and can be adjusted.

FASTING STYLE 2: *Full-day*

Full-day fasting, where a quarter of your daily calories are consumed over a full day, has become hugely popular, achieving weight-loss results where many other traditional diets have failed. It is also showing very impressive results in most of the research, working a treat on improving many health conditions such as type 2 diabetes and heart disease, as well as reducing risk factors for most major chronic diseases.

The most significant difference between full- and part-day fasting is that part-day fasting needs to be done most days, whereas full-day fasting need only be done on one, two or three days a week. Another difference is that full-day fasting requires very specific calorie counting, but only on fasting days. Unlike part-day fasting, you can eat at any point during a full-day fast, but the total calories consumed over the fasting day need to stay within 500 calories for women and 600 calories for men.

It's important to note that eating only a quarter of your daily calories can be a little hard going for some people, and consequently, compliance rates can be low and 'cheating' is common. Some people also report that they find it can impact their daily functioning and work productivity. That said, most of my patients who follow this regime report to me that they get used to their fasting periods and that their energy levels and cognition are actually fantastic on those days – some even say they feel they're buzzing!

In general, full-day fasting suits:

✓ People who tend to get engrossed in their work and 'forget' to eat through the day

✓ Individuals who are on the go all day

✓ People who travel for work: a fasting day can be done on a long-haul flight or on a day travelling interstate

✓ People who don't want to fast very often and who prefer to get their fasting 'over and done with' in a couple of days

✓ People who can't do part-day fasting because it doesn't suit their job or lifestyle

✓ Those who don't need to eat with a family or partner each day.

FULL-DAY *Fasting Comparison*

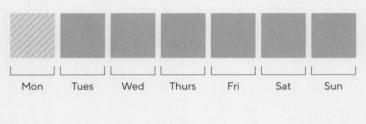

Eating   Fasting

6:1

This fasting method is the least intense of the full-day fasts as it involves fasting for just one full day of the week (any day), and eating as you normally would for the other six days. On fasting days, you eat just a quarter of your total calorie intake over the course of the day. Fasting days are flexible in that calories can be spread over the day or consumed in one or two larger meals, depending on what works best for the individual (see pages 90–91 for what to eat on fasting days).

This method is often used as a way to build up to the more intense 5:2 fasting regime. Alternatively, it is also used as a 'maintenance mode', to maintain weight or health goals that have been achieved by following the 5:2 diet for a period of time.

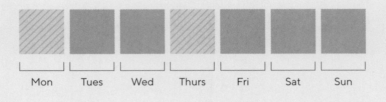

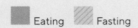 Eating   Fasting

5:2

The most popular and publicised fasting method to date
is the original 5:2 model, pioneered by Dr Michael Mosley.
For this fasting method, you eat normally for five days of
the week and fast on any two non-consecutive days that
suit you (following the same guidelines detailed
in the 6:1 fasting method).

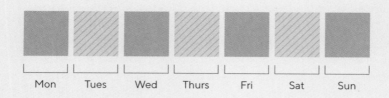

ALTERNATE-DAY FASTING

This is the most intensive fasting method, and one that shows up in a lot of the research on intermittent fasting. It is also referred to as 4:3 or 3:4 fasting, as you fast on one day then eat normally the next day, then fast the next day, and so on. In other words, fast for three or four days of the week and eat normally on the other days.

As this fasting method is the most intense, it's reasonable to expect to see more dramatic changes to weight and health markers. However, it also has the highest drop-out rate of all the fasting methods, so it's important to think twice and perhaps build up to this type of fasting regime or cycle the intensity of your fasting weeks, for example 4:3 fasting one week, then dropping down to a less intense 5:2 fast the following week.

Which days should I fast?

Very simply, it doesn't make any difference on which days you choose to fast. Fasting on non-consecutive days is easier, but you can also fast on consecutive days, if you prefer. Choosing your fasting days is very personal and also may vary from week to week, depending on what your schedule looks like and how you're feeling.

To begin with, I suggest planning for your fasting days on the weekend and scheduling your fast days for the working week. That way, you'll have plenty of time to make sure you've calculated the calories for your fasting-day meals and you'll have time to buy and prepare the food you need for the coming week.

As a general rule, I find most people prefer to fast on days when they're really busy. This way, it's easier to not think about it. I always make my fasting days ones where I'm out of the house, away from the fridge and pantry, busy in clinic or running errands so I'm distracted. I also find it's much easier if you know what food you're going to eat and when you're going to eat it. That way, not only can you can count your calories accurately, but you can also ensure there are fewer opportunities to eat outside of the food you have prepared.

Something that works for me (this is absolutely not based on any research, only my own observations and experience) is getting those full fasting days over and done with early in the week, such as on Mondays and Wednesdays. This may not work for everyone, but I find it's easier to get the fasting done at the beginning of the week; by the end, I'm looking forward to the weekend and relaxing a little.

What can I eat on my fasting days?

Unlike part-day fasting, where you can't consume any calories while fasting, a full-day fasting day does includes food; your daily intake just can't exceed more than a quarter of your total calories for the day, which is 500 calories (2,090 kj) for women and 600 calories (2,508 kj) for men.

The foods you eat when you are fasting can be anything you like, as long as it's within that calorie limit. However, I believe it's essential that you meet your basic nutritional needs. Plus, if you want to make the fasting day as easy as possible then eating certain foods that are low in calories but high in nutritional value and full of bulk will help keep you feeling fuller and more satisfied for longer. These foods include: lean proteins like eggs, skinless chicken, white fish and prawns; non-starchy vegetables like zucchini, cabbage and spinach; and low-carbohydrate fruits like berries and papaya. For a list of foods that make great go-to's on a full-fasting day, check out page 192.

The way in which you distribute the calories on a full-fasting day also doesn't matter and is completely personal. Research shows that you'll get the same results regardless of how you spread out your calories for the day. The 500/600 calories (2,090/2,508 kj) can be distributed throughout the day in three mini-meals, eaten over two moderate-sized meals in the earlier or later part of the day, or eaten all at once in one larger meal.

The most significant difference between full- and part-day fasting is that part-day fasting needs to be done most days, whereas full-day fasting need only be done on one, two or three days a week.

What can I eat on non-fasting days?

Up until now, the research on intermittent fasting has focused mostly on the fasting part and not on the eating part. The dietary recommendations for non-fasting periods are generally to 'eat what you want' as long as you're following the fasting regime.

This is all well and good in relatively short-term scientific studies, however as a long-term health strategy, there absolutely must be a focus on what is eaten when you're not fasting.

By restricting the amount of food and meal or snack opportunities you have over a week you are not only limiting the availability of calories, but also the availability of nutrients. If you spend weeks or perhaps years following a fasting regime without giving consideration to what you eat on non-fasting days, you have a high risk of developing nutrient deficiencies, such as anaemia (a result of low iron levels) and osteoporosis (brittle bones from calcium deficiency).

I certainly don't want to put the focus on weighing food, measuring portion sizes and jamming down tasteless salads – the whole point of intermittent fasting is that you can leave that diet-style mentality far behind you! I'm simply encouraging being mindful about most main meals and snacks, and aiming for a balanced and wholesome approach where real ingredients from the five food groups make up the bulk of your meals, and where processed foods high in fats and refined carbohydrates and sugars are limited. The same philosophy applies if you follow a specific dietary regime, such as vegan or gluten-free.

General nutrition guidelines to follow during your non-fasting periods:

* Follow a Mediterranean-style diet (full of fresh ingredients, healthy fats and herbs and spices).

* Eat mostly plant-based foods. About 75 per cent of your diet should come from plant foods such as vegetables, fruit, legumes, nuts, seeds and wholegrains.

* Aim for a variety of colourful fruits and vegetables each day.

* Include wholegrains such as whole wheat, barley, rye, oats, brown rice, buckwheat, amaranth, millet, spelt and quinoa in your meals.

* Include some animal-based foods such as meat, seafood and dairy – these should make up about 25 per cent of your diet. These foods provide us with essential minerals like omega 3 fatty acids, calcium, iron and zinc, vitamins such as vitamin B12 and protein. If you're vegan or vegetarian, then it's vitally important to make sure you get these nutrients from elsewhere.

* As much as possible, avoid processed (packaged) foods that have more than two or three ingredients.

How often should I fast?

How often you choose to fast comes down to your weight goals and your lifestyle. Whether you fast for one day a week or four, you will still enjoy short- and long-term health benefits. The major impact of the number of days you fast for will be metabolically, affecting your weight and fat mass.

Fasting for one day of the week might kickstart a little weight loss for some people, while for others it might be enough to keep their weight fairly stable. Fasting for two, three or four days of the week can ramp up weight loss, though this will also be dependent on what you eat on non-fasting days, your level of physical activity, age, gender and many other factors.

Patricia came to see me after a check-up with her GP revealed she was more than 20 kilograms over her normal weight. She was shocked; she'd always been about 5 kilograms over the 'normal' weight range, but she was happy and healthy there. She noticed the weight begin to creep up a few years ago, around the time she started at her current job, which requires her to travel interstate about four days a week to run workshops.

Patricia wanted to reach her weight goals, but didn't want to follow a 'diet'. She was looking for something that involved healthy and sustainable eating habits that she could follow at home, and also while travelling and staying in serviced apartments and hotels. Her medical history included elevated blood sugar levels and very low iron levels due to avoiding red meat for years.

I suggested she try the 16:8 part-day fasting method on her five working days because she could do it wherever she was, and she wouldn't have to worry about trying to find an appropriate breakfast when she was travelling. Plus, it also eliminated the very carbohydrate-dense breakfast of cereal, milk and sultanas with two milky coffees she was used to having. It also meant that when she did eat, she'd be able to be a little more flexible.

Unlike a diet, she wouldn't need to stress about not being able to meet perfect portion sizes or make sure she had balanced meals, as she often had to rely on lunches that were bought for her and order late dinners from room service. Patricia didn't drink much alcohol, so it was fine for her to continue to enjoy a few wines per week.

I did provide some nutritional guidelines for Patricia because I also wanted to make sure she was meeting her body's needs – in particular her calcium requirements, because morning fasting meant she'd be cutting out two serves of dairy. I suggested she have a milky coffee in the afternoon instead of the morning, as well as adding a serving of cheese to a sandwich at lunch if she could, as well as a small tub of yoghurt as a snack either mid-afternoon or after her dinner.

It's important to note that Patricia had also begun to tidy up her diet a little around this time. She'd cut down a lot on the chocolate she would often have when staying at hotels. She was also limiting nibbling on sweets and mints. Fasting through the morning also meant she naturally avoided the pastries that were always available at her workshops.

After two weeks of following her new part-day fasting regime Patricia had lost 2.9 kilograms and, most importantly, 4.5 cm from around her abdomen. Over the next four months she lost a total of 12 kilograms and 10 cm from around her abdomen. She's now just 5 kilograms away from her final weight goal.

Patricia is just one of many patients of mine who have benefited from using the 16:8 fasting method while travelling. Whether taking regular trips interstate for work, flying internationally for business or for long European holidays, this method is one of the easiest and most effective I have observed for maintaining weight and health goals. This is because it cuts out big buffet breakfasts or late night munching, and also limits the opportunity to eat (often fairly average) plane food.

A common complaint I hear from corporate travellers is that they are at the mercy of airport and plane food when in transit, and then being wined and dined by clients or grabbing food on the run once they reach their destination. Fasting helps them to, at the very least, maintain health goals and maintain their weight by limiting the total amount of food that they eat each day.

Another group of patients I see are those lucky enough to take an extended holiday each year. Inevitably, they resign themselves to the fact they'll gain a few kilograms on their trip. However, I've suggested that many of them try the 16:8 fasting method, which means they can maintain their weight without missing out on wine, pasta, gelato, or other local delicacies. This might mean having a late breakfast and an early dinner, or enjoying a long sleep-in, then an espresso before heading out for sightseeing, after which they can plonk themselves down hungrily in a local cafe for a delicious lunch and then a later dinner.

Patricia now reports having greater energy levels and better sleep habits. She loves not having to think about her fasting routine at all.

Setting yourself up for success

HOW TO MANAGE FASTING PERIODS

Whether your fasting involves eating a restricted number of calories over a whole day or eating nothing for part of the day, fasting can be a little uncomfortable, especially when you're just starting out. Everyone has different experiences at different times. In the same way that we're hungrier on some days than others for no apparent reason, some days you might find fasting a breeze, and other days it might be a little tougher.

Research (as well as my own clinical observations and personal experience) shows that there is a transition period after three to six weeks of fasting where the brain and body adapt to the new eating pattern. After this, fasting becomes easier and mood usually improves. The best way to navigate these rocky early weeks is to have some strategies to rely on that make your fasting periods as easy as possible.

3–6

The average number of weeks it takes for the brain and body to adapt to fasting.

TOP TIPS FOR *Successful Fasting*

✓ Be clear about why you're fasting. Is it for your health? Your mood? Your weight?

✓ Write down your reasons for fasting and your goals and refer to them if you're having a hard time getting through a fasting day.

✓ Track your moods and other physical changes because they are just as, if not more, important and 'motivating' than the number on the scale.

✓ Schedule your fasting around your social engagements. Fasting shouldn't rule your life and being able to shuffle your fasting days around, or choosing to do full-day fasts when you don't have anything on with friends and family, makes it much easier to stay on track.

✓ Plan, plan, plan your fasting periods. If you're doing a full-day fast, know exactly what you're going to eat and drink, and at what time. Make sure it's available. I can't count the number of times I've heard someone say they didn't fast on a particular day because they forgot to bring food from home so they had to go and buy something.

✓ Have plenty of water (tap or sparkling) and herbal teas available to sip on throughout your fasting period. This can help to fill you up and keep you hydrated.

✓ If you're an avid coffee or tea drinker, plan these drinks into your fasting period so it's something you can look forward to and enjoy.

✓ Keep busy! Aim to have your fasting periods over busy times in the week where you're out and about, in meetings or travelling so there's less opportunity to be tempted by food.

✓ Work your exercise around fasting periods. If you do a heavy training session early in the morning then have to fast until lunchtime, you might find that fasting period much more difficult. Aim to train later in the afternoon or evening, do a lighter session or save your heavy sessions for a 'normal' eating day.

✓ If worst comes to worst, please just eat! Some days you may just not be in the right mood or physical state for fasting and that's OK!

EXERCISE

Exercise should always be a part of a healthy lifestyle and we should all aim to do some form of activity most days of the week, not only for our body but also for our mind. If you're following a full-day fast, you may find you have less energy to work out on your fasting days. But this is very individual – many people report to me that they have a great deal of energy to exercise on fasting days, and I find this to be the case myself.

On part-day fasting days, it's a good idea to schedule exercise either just before or during your eating window. This can help to keep your appetite at bay. A common issue I encounter is that part-day fasters who exercise early in the morning can find it tough to fast until lunchtime – they are simply too hungry after their workout.

It's also common when starting a fasting regime to find that exercising on fasting days is more difficult. If this is the case for you, it's important to make sure you drink plenty of fluids before and during your exercise session, and that you bring along some food to have just in case, such as a banana. Even if you find it hard the first few times, keep in mind that most people adjust to fasting very well and eventually are able to exercise whenever they like, without it impacting on their fasting.

Whether you can only manage a gentle walk or yoga, or you prefer to do an intense, sweaty session, is really up to you. Light walking is good for your joints and your head, and a more intense session is great for your cardiovascular fitness and strength. There's a place for all types of exercise in a healthy lifestyle.

 It's early days when it comes to conclusive research about how exercising while fasting affects weight loss in humans. However, studies show that intermittent fasting might increase endurance because the body switches from using carbohydrates to fat (ketones) as a source of fuel.

Neither Lori nor Garry started fasting to lose weight. Both were already at a healthy weight, had good relationships with food and followed a very healthy diet. About three years ago, they both got into ultra-marathon running. They'd always trained regularly with a combination of gym workouts, running, swimming and cycling six days a week. Garry has a strong family history of high cholesterol, so he'd been taking statins (cholesterol-lowering medication) for many years, but then a few years ago he had decided to come off them.

Lori's medical history was slightly different; she'd been diagnosed with raised immune antibodies and coeliac disease had been questioned, but never formally diagnosed. She also had very low vitamin B12 levels and low iron, and reported she often encountered other strange health issues, such as getting sick all the time, which was unusual for her.

Both Lori and Garry had routine blood tests done and were shocked to find out that despite their healthy diet and lifestyle, Garry had raised liver enzymes (a symptom of fatty liver), and his cholesterol was very high again.

Fatty liver is when too much fat is stored in the cells of the liver. This excess fat can cause inflammation and potential damage to the liver and lead to health complications down the track. In someone who doesn't drink excessive amounts of alcohol, it is known as non-alcoholic fatty liver disease. The condition is also strongly linked with metabolic disease, which is a cluster of conditions including increased abdominal fat and raised insulin, blood pressure and triglycerides.

In clinic, one indicator we use for fatty liver is from blood tests that show elevated liver enzymes. An ultrasound can then confirm that.

Intermittent fasting can be very effective at improving and possibly reversing non-alcoholic fatty liver because it can directly target the main causes and conditions associated with it. These include visceral fat loss (the fat that sits in and around your organs), as well as helping to reduce insulin, blood pressure and triglycerides.

Like me, Lori and Garry had watched Dr Michael Mosley's documentary on 5:2 fasting and found it really interesting, but calorie counting seemed like too much work. Lori did some research and came across the 16:8 part-day fasting, which seemed far more appealing, so they began following that method five working days of the week.

Initially, Garry had a tough time – he wasn't consuming enough calories in his eating window. He was having just lunch and dinner and no afternoon snack, which meant he was almost fasting again between midday lunch and 7 pm dinner. However, he exercised in the afternoon so ultimately by adding some extra snacks, this worked out well for him.

Lori, however, trains in the morning. Generally she can still fast in the mornings except for when she's preparing for an ultra-marathon, in which case she simply stops fasting in the weeks leading up to an event in order to meet her energy requirements.

After four months of following the 16:8 fasting regime, Garry's cholesterol had returned to the normal range, his slightly elevated blood sugars were normal and his raised liver enzymes were also within the normal range. He also went from an already healthy 93 kilograms to 89 kilograms, but went down two pant sizes!

Interestingly, Lori had mostly removed gluten from her diet around this time, and it's likely that this allowed her to better absorb vitamin B12 and iron, as these levels came up to within the normal range. Her digestion was better and she was rarely unwell. The two of them also reported that they both had better concentration and cognitive function – they felt a bit 'quicker'.

After a few months of fasting, Lori also noticed she felt less anxious. She no longer felt she needed a glass of wine to wind down at the end of a day.

CAN I DRINK ALCOHOL?

Alcohol is tricky to include in any healthy lifestyle because it's very high in calories and not easily metabolised by the body. In fact, it's considered a toxin. It's also fairly well known that overdoing it with alcohol usually leads to poor diet choices, not only while drinking, but also the following day if you're not feeling your best.

Ultimately, when it comes to weight management, controlling energy intake is important. Alcoholic drinks are rich in energy (ranging from a nip of vodka at 65 calories, to as much as 300 calories for some cocktails). Compare that to a full-fasting day when a woman is limited to 500 calories and a man, 600 calories per day, and it's easy to see that's just way too many calories to be wasting on alcohol.

On a part-day fasting day, be mindful that energy you may have burned while fasting can easily be replaced by drinking too much alcohol. For example, you may have created a 500-calorie deficit on a part-day fasting day, but if you have a couple of cocktails, you can drink those calories back (and often more), making weight loss impossible.

The general recommendations for consuming alcohol are to have a few alcohol-free days per week and no more than two standard drinks for women and three for men on days that you do consume alcohol. A standard drink is one nip (30 ml) of spirits, 100–120 ml of wine or champagne, 1 middy of full-strength beer or 1 schooner (285 ml) of light beer.

COMMON FASTING *Pitfalls*

There are a few things to be mindful of when following any fasting regime:

* Overeating during the eating window or on non-fasting days, particularly when you first start out. This may cause weight to stay the same and sometimes even go up. If this is the case, adjust to a lighter regime.

* Overdoing it on black coffee, which may cause insomnia and jitteriness.

* The effects of fasting on older and elderly people are still unknown, but fasting may not be as beneficial for this group as it can be for young and middle-aged adults. Make sure you check with your doctor before embarking on a fasting regime.

* Although the research shows that in MOST cases the biochemical outcomes from fasting are positive, such as reduced cholesterol and insulin levels, in some cases the opposite happens and these may go up. Please keep a close eye on your blood test results with your doctor and adjust or cease fasting if these levels are not improving.

WHO SHOULD AVOID FASTING?

Although fasting benefits so many people, it is not for everyone. There are individuals or groups who should either seek medical support or advice before fasting, or who should avoid fasting altogether. This might be due to an unhealthy history with food or because of a vulnerable medical history that requires specialised advice and support.

Avoid fasting if you are ...

* Pregnant

* Breastfeeding

* Underweight (BMI under 20)

* Under 18 years old

* Elderly (seek advice from your medical practitioner)

Or if you ...

* Have a history of disordered eating – binge eating or restrictive eating

* Have problems controlling your blood glucose

* Suffer from fasting side-effects, like headaches, and are in a position (i.e. a truck driver or a surgeon) where you may endanger other people

* Are taking or undergoing any of the following:

    - medication for high blood glucose and insulin levels such as Metformin
    - insulin for diabetes
    - medications that need to be taken at a particular time of the day with food
    - medication for blood pressure or heart conditions
    - chemotherapy or radiotherapy.

The psychology of dieting vs. fasting

The measure of a diet's success is our ability to follow it and maintain our health and weight in the long term. Although calorie-controlled dieting can result in similar weight loss and health benefits as fasting in the short term, we know that there is a significant difference in terms of psychological impact between dieting and fasting in the long term.

As psychologist and body image expert Leanne Hall points out, many people rely on motivation to get them through a diet. The problem with this is that motivation is transient – like any other emotion such as sadness or happiness, it doesn't last. In fact, it can't be relied on long term for anything – not for keeping up exercise regimes or for staying in a job, so it definitely can't be relied on for weight management and long-term health outcomes. The petering out of motivation is commonly referred to as 'diet fatigue' and, according to Leanne, it's a real thing.

WHY DON'T TRADITIONAL DIETS WORK?

Diets promote inflexibility. They are usually something you have to stick to every day and they require a great deal of thought and adherence to rules. Typically, diets focus on restriction – whether that's of calories, foods or entire food groups. Food groups are often labelled as 'good', 'clean', 'bad' or 'fattening'; a very black-and-white approach.

1 in 6

overweight and obese adults reported maintaining weight loss of at least 10% for 1 year, at any point in their lives.

Flexibility is one of the key benefits of fasting – and so is being okay with that grey area of not eating 'perfectly' when you're not fasting.

I see this in my clinic all the time; someone tries a particular diet that involves certain rules around food, and then they try another diet that involves different rules. And when I see them years later and ask them why they're not eating dairy or why they avoid bread, they can't tell me because they don't know. Their relationship with these foods has been tarnished because at some point they've perceived them to be 'bad' or 'fattening'.

The psychological implications of continually limiting calories can be a problem, because a 'cheat meal' or a sneaky biscuit is often enough to create feelings of guilt, shame and disappointment, which can then lead to more extreme dieting behaviours. Alternatively, breaking the rules of a diet might also cause an individual to simply throw in the towel because they feel they've blown all of their good efforts, so what's the point?

Prolonged adherence to a low-calorie diet is also a concern because of increased appetite. This is the body's protective mechanism: when fuel stores get low, our system ramps up our appetite hormones to increase our food intake so we don't starve. Have you ever eaten egg whites for breakfast and a tuna salad for lunch only to devour a packet of crackers and dip, followed by pasta and ice cream later that night because you were so hungry? You can thank low blood sugar levels and hunger hormones for that.

Fasting, on the other hand, doesn't treat food the same way, though this fasting and feasting pattern is still a concern with intermittent fasting too.

THE KEY TO LONG-TERM SUCCESS

Leanne suggests approaching fasting in two ways. First, find an intrinsic or internal desire to make long-term changes to your lifestyle. Look at your health indicators: for example, have some blood tests done and check to see what your blood glucose levels, cholesterol and blood pressure are like. Look into your family medical history to determine if you are at risk of developing chronic diseases such as cancer, type 2 diabetes, heart disease, Parkinson's or Alzheimer's. Consider other physical indicators that aren't weight related – other benefits of fasting might include increased energy levels, improved immune function, joint mobility, better digestion and gut function.

The second recommendation is to make changes slowly, allowing for flexibility. As you will see later on pages 80–85, there are varying levels of intensity when it comes to fasting, and just doing a little can be better for you than doing none at all. Experimenting and building up over time is very important, not only to allow you to acclimatise physiologically to the lifestyle change, but also to allow you to get into the swing of it behaviourally.

It is the rigid rules of dieting that breed failure. Flexibility is one of the key benefits of fasting – and so is being okay with that grey area of not eating 'perfectly' when you're not fasting. Leanne says that allowing for flexibility long term can actually prevent diet cycling behaviour. She encourages embracing these shades of grey and challenging the belief that it needs to be all or nothing.

Leanne believes that monitoring your emotions and feelings, either consciously or by keeping a diary, can be an important part of maintaining a fasting regime long term. For many people, reflecting on how they are managing with their fasting regime is essential. Unlike diets, which are either 'on' or 'off', fasting can be adjusted depending on how you're feeling. So rather than just stopping, you can simply lower the intensity. This way, fasting is also still a habit. It's part of your weekly routine but you're also listening and being kind to your body and your mind. It's ultimately about valuing your health and your feelings rather than just the number on a scale.

WHEN DOES FASTING BECOME DIETING?

Fasting can start to move into the realm of dieting when it is not done properly or for the right reasons. This may be where fasting is used specifically to restrict calories or to manage emotions and in these cases it is recommended you either discontinue your fasting, or seek professional support to help you approach it in a healthier way.

Dieting also limits the opportunities for you to eat what you feel like when you want to eat it. Because diets often tell you what to eat and when, it can be difficult to enjoy your food and feel satisfied because you're eating what you have been told to or what you think you should, rather than what you really feel like. It also then limits your ability to tap into true hunger cues and decide when to eat and how much.

Intermittent fasting regimes on the other hand encourage enjoying all foods from all food groups with a focus on connecting with and getting in touch with your body and consciously deciding what you want to eat, how much and when within the non-fasting or eating window. This approach is often much more sustainable because food and meals are usually more thoroughly enjoyed and satisfying and not thought about until you're hungry again.

Getting in touch with your hunger

Another common thing I see in my work is that many people have lost touch with their hunger cues – they simply don't know when they're hungry and when they're not. If they really think about it, they are usually eating out of habit or routine, sometimes in the absence of hunger. The wonderful thing about intermittent fasting at your chosen level is that not only are there no rules around foods during your eating windows or non-fasting days (aside from eating the most nutritious food that you can), it is also a brilliant way of getting back in touch with your appetite by really feeling and experiencing hunger. Food is so much more enjoyable when you eat when you are hungry – everything tastes SO much better. The feelings of appreciation for the food, and also the satisfaction you get after eating, are much greater.

The science behind
intermittent fasting

HOW FASTING WORKS

It's not uncommon for people, whether on a diet or not, to start eating or drinking early in the morning and still be nibbling late into the night. But research suggests that eating for more than 15 hours of the day is associated with metabolic problems. This not only leads to weight gain, it can also impair the functioning of our cells and accelerate the ageing process.

Fasting, on the other hand, gives our body, specifically the energy powerhouses (aka mitochondria) in our cells, a break from processing constantly. When we eat, food moves from our stomach to our small intestine, where it begins the complex job of sending off nutrients in different directions to do their jobs within our body. The energy or calories we consume gets used right then and there to fuel our daily functions of breathing, walking, digesting, even thinking! Some fuel will also be stored as a quick-access source of energy in the form of glycogen in our muscle and liver cells. Then if we've eaten a high-calorie meal or simply consumed more energy than our body needs and there's excess energy left over, we will store that as fat in our fat (adipose) cells, causing us to gain weight. Generally though, if we eat only as much energy as our body requires, our weight will stay the same.

If it's been some time since we last ate and the glucose levels in our blood have dropped, our body then needs to access more fuel. First, it turns to the stored 'quick-access' energy from glycogen. Once those glycogen stores have been depleted, our bodies switch into 'fat-burning' mode, breaking down mostly fat stores but also some body protein (muscle) as well. Depending on your level of physical activity, humans will shift into this fat-burning mode after as little as 12 hours of fasting. In other words, fasting and restricting our energy intake periodically allows our body to access and break down stored fat, and this leads to fat loss.

METABOLIC SYNDROME

Metabolic syndrome is a modern disease characterised by a high waist measurement, insulin resistance and either high triglycerides (a type of 'bad' cholesterol) and/or high blood pressure. Metabolic syndrome greatly increases the risk of cardiovascular disease and stroke, type 2 diabetes and Alzheimer's disease. Incredibly, in animal studies, intermittent fasting was shown to reverse metabolic syndrome.

OBESITY AND WEIGHT LOSS

Obesity is a major worldwide issue that is rapidly worsening. Obesity rates have doubled since 1980, with women far more likely to be overweight than men. Many believe you can be overweight and 'healthy' (this is a very controversial topic!); whatever your opinion, there's no doubt that wide-ranging research definitively shows that carrying excess weight can have many negative health consequences. Globally, at least 2.8 million people a year die from being overweight or obese, and the risk of death increases as weight increases. The craziest thing about this statistic is that obesity can be reversed or prevented, and therefore many associated chronic diseases and, ultimately deaths, can be too. But as we've already discussed, those deaths and diseases can't be prevented if we can't figure out how to tackle weight loss effectively over the long term.

Researchers agree that the right diet for you is one that you can stick to, and certain diets work a treat for many people. My hope is that intermittent fasting is a different way of approaching and looking at weight loss that might be successful where other strategies haven't been.

3%

The average body weight lost in a study of overweight men and women following a part-day fasting regime over three months.

What the research shows

STUDIES ON FULL-DAY FASTING

* Studies of people doing 5:2 or alternate-day fasting had a loss of 4–7 per cent body weight and a 5–7 cm reduction in their waist measurement over two–three months.

* **100 overweight people lost 6 per cent of their body weight and had a 7 cm reduction in their waist measurement doing alternate-day fasting for 12 months. They also kept the weight off successfully over the six-month maintenance period.**

* In one study, post-menopausal women lost twice as much weight (11 per cent of their body weight) as pre-menopausal women.

* **A group of young overweight women doing 5:2 lost 7 per cent of their body weight and had a 4 cm reduction in their waist measurement over six months.**

* **For people within a normal weight range, one study showed that intermittent fasting can be a great way to lose those last few extra kilos. Participants lost 2–5 kilograms doing alternate-day fasting for three months.**

* Intermittent fasting maintains muscle mass better than a prolonged calorie-controlled diet. Muscle mass helps to keep our metabolism firing. The more muscle mass we have, the more energy we burn while resting. This is part of the reason why traditional weight-loss diets have a high rate of weight regain.

  – On a traditional calorie-controlled diet, for every kilogram lost, a quarter of it is muscle mass and three-quarters is fat.

  – In contrast, while doing intermittent fasting, it was found that almost all fat-free mass (muscle mass) was retained.

HEART DISEASE

High cholesterol and high blood pressure are major risk factors for heart disease. Cholesterol is a fat that is carried around in our blood. Low density lipoprotein (LDL) is the main source of cholesterol that can build up and cause a hardening of plaque in the arteries, which can lead to heart attack.

All methods of intermittent fasting have been shown to reduce blood pressure, improve cholesterol profiles and protect against heart disease.

What the research shows

STUDIES ON PART-DAY FASTING

* Cholesterol: Obese study participants following 16:8 had a 15 per cent drop in triglycerides in three months.

* **Cholesterol: A study of young men over two months following 16:8 had an increase in their 'good' high density lipoprotein (HDL) cholesterol by 10 per cent.**

* Blood pressure: Obese men and women who followed 16:8 for three months had a reduction in blood pressure.

STUDIES ON FULL-DAY FASTING

* **Cholesterol: A 12-month study on alternate-day fasting showed that it helped decrease triglycerides by 25 per cent and increase 'good' HDL cholesterol by 10 per cent.**

* Cholesterol: A study of young overweight women showed that following 5:2 for six months reduced their LDL cholesterol by 10 per cent and triglycerides by 15 per cent.

* **Blood pressure: Alternate-day and 5:2 fasting was shown to reduce blood pressure in overweight and normal weight adults.**

Matthew is a 45-year-old father of three. He has always been in good health and has a lean build. During his annual insurance health check for work, his blood test results came back showing that his cholesterol levels, particularly his triglycerides, were in the high range. In this scenario, it is common for some people to start on cholesterol-lowering medications (statins), particularly if they have other high cardiovascular disease risk factors. However, Matthew's GP suggested he trial a diet and lifestyle change first to see if he could reduce his cholesterol himself and avoid taking statins.

Matthew came to see me and after taking a comprehensive look at his habits, it was clear that his diet was quite healthy and he exercised regularly. Matthew was also in a normal weight range but his waist measurement was 2–3 cm more than recommended. Basically, there wasn't a whole lot of room to move when it came to making changes to his diet.

I suggested he trial part-day fasting on his workdays for two months, eating between lunch and dinner so he could eat the evening meal with his family. After that time, we would have his bloods retested to check his cholesterol levels.

Two months later, Matthew's total cholesterol and triglyceride levels had returned to well within the normal range and he had lost 3.5 cm from around his waist, indicating a loss of abdominal fat.

Matthew now maintains his weight and his normal cholesterol levels by part-day fasting for three days of the week.

Matthew's GP suggested he trial a diet and lifestyle change to see if he could reduce his cholesterol himself and avoid taking statins.

TYPE 2 DIABETES

Type 2 diabetes occurs when the body becomes resistant to the normal effects of insulin and can no longer process the glucose in the blood. Pre-diabetes is when blood glucose levels are higher than normal but not high enough to be classified as diabetes. This may also include insulin resistance, which is where cells don't recognise or respond to insulin and so glucose isn't taken from the blood and into the cells properly. When this occurs, the pancreas then produces more insulin to compensate.

Current research shows that intermittent fasting can yield incredible results when it comes to tackling blood glucose levels. It can help to improve glucose control and therefore may prevent or slow down the progression of pre-diabetes into type 2 diabetes. Some scientists are going as far as saying that intermittent fasting can 'reverse' type 2 diabetes.

Preliminary findings show part-day fasting has similar results to full-day fasting, with significant reductions in insulin and blood glucose levels.

What the research shows

STUDIES ON PART-DAY FASTING

* Young men who followed 16:8 for two months had a 40 per cent decrease in insulin resistance.

20%

The reduction in insulin levels in a study tracking non-diabetic obese adults doing both 5:2 and alternate-day fasting.

STUDIES ON FULL-DAY FASTING

* **The most significant results were seen in individuals with pre-diabetes doing alternate-day fasting – over 12 months they had a 30 per cent decrease in insulin levels.**

* Another study showed a 20–25 per cent reduction in insulin resistance in otherwise healthy overweight adults, and up to 45 per cent in another study in people with pre-diabetes.

CANCER

Up until now, most research on the link between intermittent fasting and cancer has been conducted on animals, however this can still be helpful as it gives us a preliminary understanding as to the effects it may have on humans. A lot of research is still needed to confirm the effects of fasting on cancer in humans.

What the research shows

STUDIES ON PART-DAY FASTING

* Fasting can reduce the recurrence of breast cancer in women who fasted for longer than 13 hours overnight.

ANIMAL STUDIES RELATING TO FASTING AND CANCER

* **Fasting can slow the growth of tumours in breast and prostate tissue.**

* Fasting can induce autophagy, which is the body's process to clean up damaged cellular components and prevent the development of tumours in malfunctioning cells.

50%

In animals, fasting can reduce insulin-like growth factor (ILG-1), which promotes the growth of cancer cells, by as much as 50%.

BRAIN HEALTH

Fasting is thought to be a promising way of preventing neurodegenerative diseases. It's thought that fasting 'shocks' the cells in the brain, and that this process stimulates the creation of new neurons. When we are in fasting mode, our body produces a protein called brain-derived neurotrophic factor (BDNF), which also stimulates the growth of new neurons and the connections between neurons.

What the research shows

* These new neurons and neuronal connections have also been shown to be more resistant to plaque accumulation, which is the major cause of both Alzheimer's and Parkinson's disease.

* **Fasting can also help to improve mental clarity and focus, though perhaps not to begin with. Veterans of fasting often report that they feel very sharp and energetic on fasting days and have increased alertness and mental awareness. This is believed to be due to the release of a hormone called catecholamine during fasting.**

* Full-day 5:2 fasting has been shown to support brain health by improving memory and cognition and helping to protect against neurodegenerative diseases like Alzheimer's and Parkinson's.

INFLAMMATION

Chronic inflammation is associated with the increased risk of some diseases and conditions. Inflammation is the body's immune response to damage or unwanted pathogens. It's very helpful when you cut your finger or bang your knee because your immune system leaps into action to repair the damage. But when the inflammation sticks around for longer periods, it becomes chronic inflammation, which can eventually trigger diseases and conditions such as rheumatoid arthritis, atherosclerosis and some cancers.

What the research shows

* Researchers have found that intermittent fasting produces a compound that blocks a part of the inflammatory response involved in some inflammatory disorders such as type 2 diabetes, heart disease and Alzheimer's, as well as some autoinflammatory disorders.

GUT HEALTH

During a fasting period, it's not only our cells that get a break but also the bacteria in our gut. Fasting gives our gastrointestinal system time to heal and repair. The bacteria in our gut are known collectively as the microbiome, and a healthy microbiome plays a very important role in our overall health – from our digestion to our immune system – protecting us against pathogens.

What the research shows

* Studies have shown that fasting not only has the potential to restore normal gut microbiota, it can also help some beneficial bacterial colonies to thrive, and therefore increase microbial diversity.

Sandra came to see me for some weight-loss advice. She was 30 kilograms heavier than her ideal weight and the heaviest she'd been in her life. This really concerned her because she's heading towards menopause, when weight can be even harder to lose and keep off.

Sandra is a writer and she does her best work late in the evening. She often gets up with her partner and teenage son around 7.30 am and has toast and a coffee. She begins her work day around 10 am at a cafe, where she eats a full breakfast of egg and toast and a green juice. She then goes on to have lunch around 1 pm, an afternoon snack, and early dinner with her family around 6.30 pm. Then, as everyone is settling down, she works and gets the munchies so she will often eat something, whether it's leftover dinner, a bread roll, rice cakes or chocolate at 10 pm. If she's still up at 12 or 1 am, she'll eat then, too.

The problem, I explained to Sandra, was not necessarily the type of food she was eating but how long her eating day was. Because she wakes reasonably early but stays up quite late, she is effectively eating one-and-a-half days' worth of food in one 24-hour period, with often just a seven-hour window of time overnight where she is not eating.

Sandra and I had a long discussion about this and we formulated a plan that she simply needed to begin by limiting her eating day to 12 hours. I suggested that the toast (with butter and Vegemite) first thing in the morning wasn't necessary, nor was it terribly nutritious. She realised she wasn't actually hungry at that time anyway; she was just eating because her partner and son were.

This then allowed for her eating day to begin at the cafe at 10 am, which meant she needed to be finished eating by 10 pm. In that time, she could then go on to have lunch around 2 pm, an early dinner at around 6.30 pm, and then enjoy a snack at around 9.30 or 10 pm before beginning her fast again. However, if she was working later than that, she could enjoy herbal teas and decaf black coffee.

I spoke to Sandra a month later and she had experienced an interesting start to her journey. She explained feeling as though she was in a 'food panic' – she found she was overcompensating and eating more in her 12-hour eating window and, as a result, she'd gained a kilo. Since then, she's identified and workshopped her response and reports she is now doing very well and losing around a kilogram per week. Even better, she's finding the fasting program no problem to follow now that she's in the swing of it.

> **The problem, I explained to Sandra, was not necessarily the type of food she was eating, but how long her eating day was.**

AGEING

Researchers are finding that the combination of exercise and intermittent fasting can slow ageing, as well as the onset of diseases related to ageing, by improving the way our cells adapt to stress. But more research is needed in this area of fasting to gain a better understanding of its effect on our longevity.

What the research shows

GENERAL DATA RELATING TO FASTING AND AGEING

* Fasting is believed to promote healthy ageing by reducing certain biochemical markers, which collectively are associated with a faster ageing process.

STUDIES ON FULL-DAY FASTING

* In an animal study, rats that fasted for 24 hours, twice a week (a modified form of 5:2 fasting, as this version involves no calories at all for 24 hours) had a significant increase in lifespan. When evaluating the research, it's important to note that these positive outcomes were related to younger and middle-aged animals. For older animals, fasting had no effect or even a negative effect on their ageing process.

CASE STUDY
Celia: DIABETIC AND OVERWEIGHT

Celia reluctantly started seeing me after her GP insisted she address her uncontrolled type 2 diabetes and high weight. Diagnosed with type 2 diabetes around 10 years ago, she checks her blood glucose levels several times throughout the day. Despite taking a high level of diabetes medication, she has consistently high blood glucose readings. Long term, this can damage the small capillaries in the hands and feet (causing numbness), behind the eyes (affecting sight) and in the kidneys (causing kidney damage). Celia's weight was also in the morbidly obese range, which, coupled with type 2 diabetes, dramatically increased her risk for developing other chronic diseases like heart disease.

Celia had tried every diet, from popular weight-loss programs to shakes, detoxes and tablets. She always felt resentful, restricted, hungry and miserable when following these programs, and would break her diet within weeks.

I suggested easing into some changes very slowly by following the least 'diety' approach, and part-day fasting for just a few days of the week to get a feel for it. The goal was to hopefully build that up to five or even seven days of part-day fasting a week. Reluctantly she agreed, but her biggest concern was not being able to go out in the morning and have her latte. We discussed her having black coffee and tea and herbal teas and then she could break her fast around 11 am with a latte, have lunch at her normal time of 1 pm and then start fasting again from 7 pm.

Celia left my office and I had a chat with her GP afterwards to recap on our session. I told him I'd be surprised if she returned to see me, let alone followed the fasting regime I had suggested. To my surprise and delight, Celia did return to see me, and has done so every month now for the last four. She is in fact fasting for five or six days a week and has lost 10 kilograms so far. Every blood glucose reading she has taken and logged for me to see has been within the normal range. She is so set into the rhythm of her fasting regime she reports she doesn't even think about it anymore.

Celia's goals are now focused on reducing her medications. She said to me in one of our sessions, 'I don't want to be skinny, I just want to feel more comfortable.'

> **Celia had tried every diet ... She felt resentful, restricted, hungry and miserable when following these programs, and would break her diet within weeks.**

Putting fasting into practice

The great thing about fasting is that it is very flexible and can be tailored to your lifestyle and your weekly schedule. Some people prefer to decide on a weekly routine that works for them and then stick to it no matter what is going on. This may be easier if you've got a weekly schedule that rarely changes and if you get to work at the same time each day and tend to stay in the one location.

Others have weekly schedules that change, either because they travel for work, attend seminars or work in shifts, or because they're juggling commitments such as deadlines, vacations, functions or school holidays. A traditional weight-loss diet would be impossible to follow with such a varied schedule and would end just as quickly as it started. Intermittent fasting allows you to look at the coming week and simply choose how you're going to fast based on what you have on.

A majority of the research that has been done on intermittent fasting so far has been on clinically obese people (with a BMI greater than 35). Naturally these participants saw significant changes to their health and their weight because their starting weight was high. When you embark on any health or weight journey, it's important that you look at your baseline diet and exercise regime. If your weight is already clinically normal (a BMI between 20 and 25), then weight loss can be tricky because your body will want to maintain that weight. Also, if the changes you're making are not too dissimilar to your current regime, you may not see much of a change.

Intermittent fasting allows you to look at the coming week and simply choose how you're going to fast based on what you have on.

STRUCTURING YOUR FASTING REGIME

Before deciding on the approach you're going to follow, take 5 minutes on the weekend to look at your diary for the week ahead. Plan when and how you are going to fast. Things to take into consideration might include:

WORK

* Hours spent at work:

....

* Time spent commuting to and from work:

....

* Will you be in an office, on the road or off-site?

....

MEETINGS

* Will these be in cafes, closed rooms or off-site?

....

* Are they likely to run over their allocated time?

....

* Will food be provided or should you bring your own?

....

TRAVELLING

* Time spent at airports:

....

* Food provided in-flight or in airport lounges:

....

* Where will you be eating when you reach your destination? Will you be dining out or getting room service?

....

WHEN DO YOU PLAN TO EXERCISE?

* Does this need to be scheduled during a fasting or an eating window?

....

* Can you exercise on a fasting day, or is a non-fasting day better for you?

....

WHO WILL YOU BE EATING WITH?

☐ Partner or flatmate who is/isn't fasting

☐ Kids or family who might want or need to eat differently to you

☐ Friends or colleagues at meals out, work functions or social events

WHICH LEVEL OF FASTING INTENSITY IS RIGHT FOR YOU?

There are many levels of fasting intensity, and these can even be mixed and matched throughout a week, if you like. You might want to start with the gentlest fasting style and ramp up from there, or you may want to choose the style that easily slots into your weekly routine.

Another great way of deciding on your plan is to evaluate your health and weight goals and work back from there. If you are set on losing a specific amount of weight by a certain point in time or on improving certain health markers, a more intense fasting style that yields a greater weekly calorie deficit (such as the alternate-day fasting method) may be a good option in the short term. Those first couple of weeks will be a challenge, but it will get easier. And once your goals are achieved, you can always move into maintenance mode with a gentler fasting style.

WHAT ARE YOU TRYING TO ACHIEVE?	FASTING APPROACH
General health and weight maintenance	A mild approach such as part-day fasting a few days a week, or just one full-day fast a week
Weight loss of 1–5 kilograms	A mild to moderate approach such as three to seven days a week of part-day fasting OR one to two full-day fasts OR a combination of two to three part-day fasts and one full-day fast
Weight loss of more than 5 kilograms	A moderate to intense approach of five to seven days a week of part-day fasting OR two to four full-day fasts OR a combination of two full-day fasts and two to three part-day fasts

Fasting methods for weight-loss goals

The amount of energy our bodies need each day and the rate at which we burn it varies from person to person and can even change from day to day. Our daily energy requirements depend on our gender, age, activity level and even the environment in our gut, as well as many other factors. If you are curious to find out roughly how much energy you need each day to maintain your weight, there are many great online calculators that calculate your total daily energy expenditure (TDEE).

Although everyone's exact numbers are going to be specific to them, generally speaking in order to lose 1 kilogram of fat we need a deficit of 7,000 calories (29,260 kj). If you want to get a rough idea of what to expect with your weight loss, I've included approximate numbers for each method of fasting, so you have an idea of the kind of calorie deficit you could expect when following these methods. Please remember, these are estimates only, and actual calorie deficits will vary from person to person.

ON A 5:2 *Fasting Day*

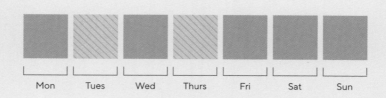

Mon   Tues   Wed   Thurs   Fri   Sat   Sun

■ Eating   ▨ Fasting

* **A woman eating 500 calories (2,090 kj) could expect a deficit of around 1,500 calories (6,279 kj)**

* **A man eating 600 calories (2,508 kj) could expect a deficit of around 1,800 calories (7,524 kj)**

By fasting for two days of the week, a woman could expect to lose just under half a kilogram per week (two days x 1,500 calories = 3,000 calories/12,552 kj). A man could expect to lose just over half a kilogram per week (two days x 1,800 calories = 3,600 calories/15,062 kj). As with part-day fasting, the more activity done, the greater the fat-burning capacity.

PART-DAY *Fasting Comparison*

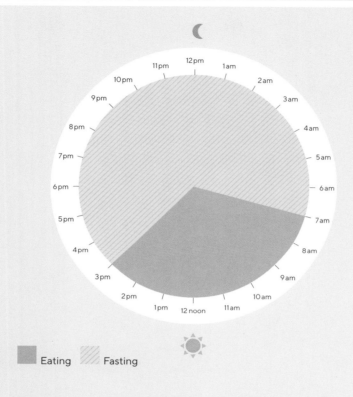

Eating   Fasting

* **A woman could expect a deficit of around 500 calories (2,090 kj)**

* **A man could expect a deficit of around 600 calories (2,508 kj)**

So for example, a woman part-day fasting five days a week (five days x 500 calories) could expect to be in energy deficit of 2,500 calories (10,460 kj), and a man following the same regime (five days x 600 calories) could expect an energy deficit of 3,000 calories (12,540 kj). Both of these examples are just under half a kilogram of weight loss. By including exercise during this week, they can increase their energy deficit and weight loss.

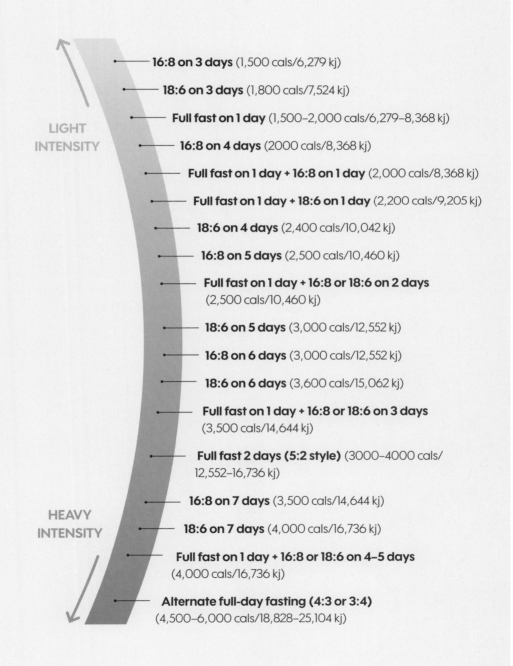

LIGHT INTENSITY

16:8 on 3 days (1,500 cals/6,279 kj)

18:6 on 3 days (1,800 cals/7,524 kj)

Full fast on 1 day (1,500–2,000 cals/6,279–8,368 kj)

16:8 on 4 days (2000 cals/8,368 kj)

Full fast on 1 day + 16:8 on 1 day (2,000 cals/8,368 kj)

Full fast on 1 day + 18:6 on 1 day (2,200 cals/9,205 kj)

18:6 on 4 days (2,400 cals/10,042 kj)

16:8 on 5 days (2,500 cals/10,460 kj)

Full fast on 1 day + 16:8 or 18:6 on 2 days (2,500 cals/10,460 kj)

18:6 on 5 days (3,000 cals/12,552 kj)

16:8 on 6 days (3,000 cals/12,552 kj)

18:6 on 6 days (3,600 cals/15,062 kj)

Full fast on 1 day + 16:8 or 18:6 on 3 days (3,500 cals/14,644 kj)

Full fast 2 days (5:2 style) (3000–4000 cals/12,552–16,736 kj)

16:8 on 7 days (3,500 cals/14,644 kj)

18:6 on 7 days (4,000 cals/16,736 kj)

Full fast on 1 day + 16:8 or 18:6 on 4–5 days (4,000 cals/16,736 kj)

Alternate full-day fasting (4:3 or 3:4) (4,500–6,000 cals/18,828–25,104 kj)

HEAVY INTENSITY

Meal plans for
fasting days

Many of the people I see in my practice as a dietitian like to have guidelines they can refer to when starting on a new fasting regime. For that reason, on the next few pages you'll find different fasting options and sample meal plans for these using the recipes in this book. You don't have to stick to these rigidly; they are here to give you inspiration on days you might be stuck for ideas. They are also good examples of what a balanced week looks like, in terms of the mix of ingredients and meals.

PART-DAY FASTING OPTIONS

Exactly when you fast and eat on a part-day fasting day is up to you. Choose an eight-hour window that's best for you to eat in or, perhaps more importantly, choose a 16-hour window of time that works best for you to fast in. Here are four of the most common part-day fasting scenarios, with sample meal plans for each so you can see how a day might look.

Eat breakfast and fast from 3 pm

This will be ideal for people who rely on breakfast to kickstart their day, and also for singles who don't have to eat dinner with a family or partner at set times. This option is also great for people working long hours who typically turn to toast or takeaways for their dinner.

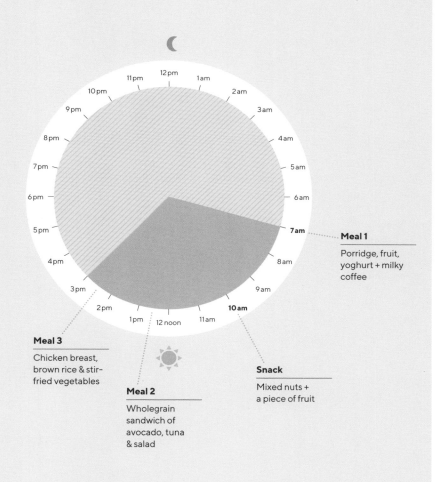

Meal 1
Porridge, fruit, yoghurt + milky coffee

Snack
Mixed nuts + a piece of fruit

Meal 2
Wholegrain sandwich of avocado, tuna & salad

Meal 3
Chicken breast, brown rice & stir-fried vegetables

 Eating Fasting

Brunch and an early dinner

This option is ideal for those who can skip breakfast but can't quite get through to lunchtime without eating. It's also great for people who are able to take a break mid-morning or eat at their desk, as well as parents who like to eat dinner early with their kids.

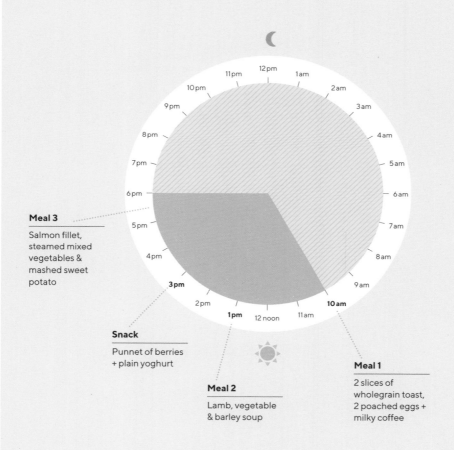

Meal 3

Salmon fillet, steamed mixed vegetables & mashed sweet potato

Snack

Punnet of berries + plain yoghurt

Meal 2

Lamb, vegetable & barley soup

Meal 1

2 slices of wholegrain toast, 2 poached eggs + milky coffee

 Eating  Fasting

Fast until lunchtime and eat a later dinner

This plan is ideal for chronic breakfast skippers, or those who can go through to lunchtime easily without eating. It also suits those who often find themselves racing into work late and grabbing pastries, muffins or other less-healthy breakfast options on the way. It's great for corporate workers or shift workers who tend to eat dinner late in the evening.

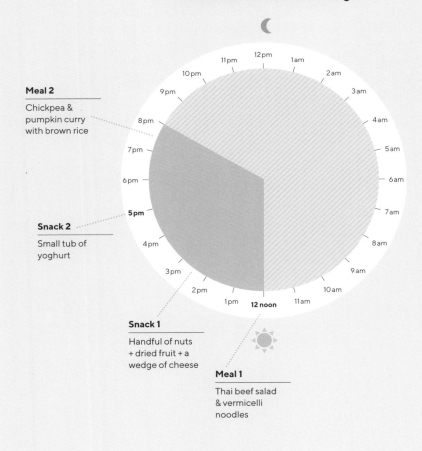

Meal 2
Chickpea & pumpkin curry with brown rice

Snack 2
Small tub of yoghurt

Snack 1
Handful of nuts + dried fruit + a wedge of cheese

Meal 1
Thai beef salad & vermicelli noodles

Eating   Fasting

FULL-DAY FASTING OPTIONS

How you distribute your calories over the day (500 calories/2,090 kj for women, 600 calories/2,508 kj for men) is very personal and may require some trial and error. Like part-day fasting, you may find that how you distribute your calories will make or break your day. My suggestion is to have a good think about your routine and identify when you're hungriest, or if you'd like to continue having certain meals with your family or partner and then make your decision from there.

You might be someone who needs a little something at each main meal, in which case you may want to distribute your calories over the three main meals of the day. This is possible, but I will add that this is reported as being one of the hardest strategies because it's a little like teasing yourself with small portions of food constantly through the day. If you can hold off until lunchtime, then you can distribute your calories between lunch and dinner, which (in my experience) is the most popular and usually the most manageable strategy to stick with. Here are a few ideas of how you might structure a day – these are just suggestions. I've also created full weekly meal plans (see page 92) if you prefer more detailed guidance.

OPTION 1: *Distributing your calories across the day*

TIME OF DAY	FEMALE (500 CALORIES/2,090 KJ)	MALE (600 CALORIES/2,508 KJ)
7 am	Black coffee with 25 ml skim milk (10 cals/42 kj) 1 slice of wholegrain toast + 1 boiled egg (160 cals/669 kj)	Black coffee with 25 ml skim milk (10 cals/42 kj) 1 slice of wholegrain toast + 1 boiled egg (160 cals/669 kj)
10 am	Black coffee with 25 ml skim milk (10 cals/42 kj)	Black coffee with 25 ml skim milk (10 cals/42 kj)
12 pm	2 cups chopped mixed salad vegetables (80 cals/335 kj) + 100 g unprocessed shaved chicken breast (105 cals/439 kj)	2 cups chopped mixed salad vegetables (80 cals/335 kj) + 100 g unprocessed shaved chicken breast (105 cals/439 kj)
3 pm	Tea with 25 ml skim milk (10 cals/42 kj)	Tea with 25 ml skim milk (10 cals/42 kj)
6 pm	2 cups vegetable & lentil soup (120 cals/502 kj)	2 cups vegetable & lentil soup (120 cals/502 kj) + 1 slice of wholegrain toast (100 cals/418 kj)
TOTAL	495 CALORIES/2,071 KJ	595 CALORIES/2,489 KJ

OPTION 2: *Have your calories across half the day*

TIME OF DAY	FEMALE (500 CALORIES/2,090 KJ)	MALE (600 CALORIES/2,508 KJ)
7 am	Black coffee (0 cals)	Black coffee (0 cals)
10 am	Black coffee (0 cals)	Black coffee (0 cals)
1 pm	Mixed salad (80 cals/335 kj) + 1 small tin of tuna in olive oil, drained (110 cals/460 kj) + 1 tablespoon low-fat cottage cheese (20 cals/84 kj)	Mixed salad (80 cals/335 kj) + 1 small tin of tuna in olive oil, drained (110 cals/460 kj) + 1 tablespoon low-fat cottage cheese (20 cals/84 kj) + 2 Ryvitas (70 cals/293 kj)
3 pm	No-added-sugar yoghurt (95 cals/397 kj)	No-added-sugar yoghurt (95 cals/397 kj)
7 pm	150 g prawn meat (130 cals/544 kj) + 150 g bunch of bok choy (30 cals/125 kj) stir-fried with 1 teaspoon olive oil (40 cals/167 kj) + 1 tablespoon tamari sauce (15 cals/63 kj) + fresh chilli flakes	150 g prawn meat (130 cals/544 kj) + 150 g bunch of bok choy (30 cals/125 kj) stir-fried with 1 teaspoon olive oil (40 cals/167 kj) + 1 tablespoon tamari sauce (15 cals/63 kj) + fresh chilli flakes
TOTAL	520 CALS/2,176 KJ	590 CALS/2,468 KJ

OPTION 3: *Save all your calories for one meal*

TIME OF DAY	FEMALE (500 CALORIES/2,090 KJ)	MALE (600 CALORIES/2,508 KJ)
7 am	Black coffee with 25 ml full-fat milk (15 cals/63 kj)	Black coffee with 25 ml full-fat milk (15 cals/63 kj)
10 am	Black coffee with 25 ml full-fat milk (15 cals/63 kj)	Black coffee with 25 ml full-fat milk (15 cals/63 kj)
12 pm	Green tea (0 cals)	Green tea (0 cals)
3 pm	Tea with 25 ml full-fat milk (15 cals/63 kj)	Tea with 25 ml full-fat milk (15 cals/63 kj)
6 pm	200 g lean eye fillet steak (290 cals/1,213 kj) + ½ cup green peas (55 cals/230 kj) + 1 cup steamed broccoli (50 cals/209 kj) + 1 orange (70 cals/293 kj) for dessert.	250 g lean eye fillet steak (360 cals/1,505 kj) + 1 cup green peas (110 cals/460 kj) + 1 cup steamed broccoli (50 cals/209 kj) + 1 small apple (50 cals/ 209 kj) for dessert
TOTAL	510 CALORIES/2,132 KJ	615 CALORIES/2,573 KJ

16:8 FASTING *on seven days of the week*

	MONDAY	TUESDAY	WEDNESDAY
	FASTING		
BREAKFAST	Black tea/ coffee + water	Black tea/ coffee + water	Black tea/ coffee + water
MORNING SNACK	Herbal tea + water	Herbal tea + water	Herbal tea + water
LUNCH	Leftover Bunless Lamb and Mushroom Burger (p. 126) (from Sunday night)	Leftover Quick Salmon with Mixed Veg Mash (p. 160)	Leftover Korean Beef Bibimbap (p. 142)
AFTERNOON SNACK	Tea/coffee + a piece of fruit + handful of nuts	Tea/coffee + 2 bliss balls + wholegrain crackers & cheese	Tea/coffee +small fruit salad + chopped veggie sticks & hummus
DINNER	Quick Salmon with Mixed Veg Mash (p. 160)	Korean Beef Bibimbap (p. 142)	Prawn Tom Yum Soup (p. 152)
EVENING SNACK	Small tub of yoghurt	Berries & yoghurt	Homemade chai tea
	FASTING		

THURSDAY	FRIDAY	SATURDAY	SUNDAY
FASTING			
Black tea/ coffee + water	Black tea/ coffee + water	Black tea/ coffee + water	Black tea/ coffee + water
Herbal tea + water	Herbal tea + water	Herbal tea + water	Herbal tea + water
Leftover Prawn Tom Yum Soup (p. 152)	Garlic Mixed Seafood Noodles (p. 156)	Smoked Salmon Anytime Wrap (p. 116)	Turmeric Scrambled Tofu and Peas (p. 118)
Tea/coffee + small tub of yoghurt + sprinkle of seeds & coconut	Tea/coffee + good-quality corn chips & guacamole	Tea/coffee + wholegrain crackers & cheese	Tea/coffee + small tub of yoghurt
Warm Chickpea and Cauliflower Salad with Honey Roasted Carrots (p. 179)	Chunky Chicken and Vegetable Soup (p. 130)	Italian Seafood Stew (p. 158)	Bunless Lamb and Mushroom Burger (p. 126)
Wedge of cheese + handful of nuts	Homemade hot chocolate	Dark chocolate	A piece of fruit
FASTING			

FULL-DAY FASTING (5:2)

Eating normally for five days and full-day fasting on two days

	MONDAY	TUESDAY	WEDNESDAY
	FASTING DAY 500/600 calories (2,090/2,508 kj)	**NORMAL DAY**	**FASTING DAY** 500/600 calories (2,090/2,508 kj)
BREAKFAST	Small skim milk latte (60 cals/249 kj) + water	Mixed Berry Breakfast Parfait (p. 106)	Small skim milk latte (60 cals/249 kj) + water
MORNING SNACK	Herbal tea + water	Tea/ coffee + 2 bliss balls	Herbal tea + water
LUNCH	*5:2 recipe option: Smashed Avo on Toast (170 cals/711 kj) (p. 120)	Leftover Fish Tacos with Cabbage Salad (p. 164)	*5:2 recipe option: Beef Pho (110 cals/460 kj) (p. 138)
AFTERNOON SNACK	A small piece of fruit (apple, orange, peach) (see p. 194) (50 cals/209 kj)	Tea/ coffee + wholegrain crackers & cheese	50 g berries (25 cals/105 kj) + small tub no added sugar yoghurt (100 cals/418 kj)
DINNER	*5:2 recipe option: Fish Tacos with Cabbage Salad (255 cals/1066 kj) (p. 164)	Beef Pho (p. 138)	*5:2 recipe option: Prawn Pad Thai (220 cals/920 kj) (p. 146)
EVENING SNACK	Herbal tea	Berries & yoghurt	Herbal tea

THURSDAY	FRIDAY	SATURDAY	SUNDAY
NORMAL DAY	**NORMAL DAY**	**NORMAL DAY**	**NORMAL DAY**
Smashed Avo on Toast with Feta and Chilli (p. 120)	Chewy Banana and Oat Breakfast Cookies (p. 109)	Mexican Black Bean and Corn Frittata (p. 113)	Choc-coconut Chia Puddings (p. 104)
Tea/ coffee + a piece of fruit	Tea/ coffee + wholegrain crackers & avocado	Tea/ coffee	Tea/ coffee
Leftover Prawn Pad Thai (p. 146)	Leftover Nasi Goreng (p. 169)	Vegan Grazing Platter (p. 173)	French-style Vegetable and Lentil Soup (p. 170)
Tea/ coffee + small tub of yoghurt + sprinkle of seeds & coconut	Tea/ coffee + good-quality corn chips + guacamole	Tea/ coffee + a piece of fruit	Tea/ coffee + small tub of yoghurt
Nasi Goreng (p. 169)	Capricciosa Pizzas (p. 136)	Eggplant & Ricotta 'Cannelloni' (p. 182)	'Sort of' Spaghetti and Turkey Meatballs (p. 129)
Wedge of cheese + handful of nuts	Homemade hot chocolate	Chocolate-coated strawberries	A piece of fruit

COMBINATION OF *Part-day and Full-day fasting*

One full-day fasting day and four part-day fasting days

	MONDAY	TUESDAY	WEDNESDAY
	FASTING DAY 500/600 calories (2,090/2,508 kj)	**NORMAL DAY**	**PART-DAY FAST**
BREAKFAST	Small skim milk latte (60 cals/249 kj) + water	Zoats (Zucchini Oats) (p. 102)	Black tea/ coffee + water
MORNING SNACK	Herbal tea + water	Tea/ coffee + 2 bliss balls	Herbal tea + water
LUNCH	*5:2 option: Baked Peach Crumble (260 cals/1087 kj) (p. 110)	Vegan Super Bowl (p. 186)	Israeli Cauliflower 'Rice' with Felafels (p. 174)
AFTERNOON SNACK	Black tea/ coffee/ herbal tea + water	Tea/ coffee + wholegrain crackers & cheese	Tea/ coffee + small fruit salad + chopped veggie sticks + hummus
DINNER	*5:2 option: Tandoori Fish with Cumin-spiced Basmati Rice (265 cals/1108 kj) (p. 150)	Honey Soy Pork Tenderloin (p. 140)	Salmon and Pumpkin Fish Burgers (p. 148)
EVENING SNACK	Herbal tea	Berries & yoghurt	Homemade chai tea

THURSDAY	FRIDAY	SATURDAY	SUNDAY
PART-DAY FAST	**PART-DAY FAST**	**PART-DAY FAST**	**NORMAL DAY**
Black tea/ coffee + water	Black tea/ coffee + water	Black tea/ coffee + water	Japanese Cabbage Omelette (p.114)
Herbal tea + water	Herbal tea + water	Herbal tea + water	Water
Tuna Nicoise Salad (p. 163)	Creamy Tuna Salad (p. 154)	DIY Chicken Teriyaki Hand Rolls (p. 135)	Mexican Turkey Stuffed Capsicums (p. 132)
Tea/ coffee + small tub of yoghurt + sprinkle of seeds & coconut	Tea/ coffee + good-quality corn chips + guacamole	Tea/ coffee + wholegrain crackers & cheese	Tea/ coffee + small tub of yoghurt
Mediterranean Haloumi Salad (p. 176)	Chicken San Choy Bau (p. 124)	Whole Roasted Cauliflower with Mushroom Sauce (p. 185)	Four-Bean Chilli with Mountain Bread Nachos (p. 180)
Wedge of cheese + handful of nuts	Homemade hot chocolate	Dark chocolate	A piece of fruit

PART TWO
recipes

Enjoy a varied range of wholefoods, rich in flavour and nutrients.

breakfast

Zoats
(Zucchini Oats)

Serves 2

80 g (⅔ cup) rolled oats

2 teaspoons black or white
chia seeds

1 zucchini, coarsely grated

3 tablespoons unsweetened almond
milk (see page 192)

1 green apple, peeled, cored and
coarsely grated

Honey, to serve

2 kiwi fruit, peeled and sliced,
to serve

Zucchini in oats? OK, I hear you, but I promise you won't even know it's in there. It adds great texture and bulks out the dish beautifully, plus it adds some extra nutrition to your morning.

1. Place the oats, chia seeds, zucchini and 375 ml (1½ cups) water in a small saucepan and mix together well. Place over a low heat and slowly bring to a simmer over 5–10 minutes. Stir occasionally to make sure it's not catching on the bottom.
2. Once the porridge has thickened and has reached your desired consistency, stir in the almond milk. Turn off the heat, then stir in the grated apple.
3. Divide between two bowls and serve drizzled with honey and topped with slices of kiwi fruit.

Choc-coconut Chia Puddings

Serves 2

3 tablespoons black or white chia seeds

250 ml (1 cup) unsweetened almond and coconut milk (see page 192)

2 heaped teaspoons cacao or cocoa powder

1 tablespoon desiccated coconut + 2 teaspoons extra, to serve

1 heaped tablespoon coconut yoghurt + extra, to serve

2 drops stevia concentrate

Raspberries, to serve

This lovely little dish reminds me of a chocolate mousse, but with a more nutritious and calorie-controlled twist.

1. Place the chia seeds, almond and coconut milk, cacao, desiccated coconut, yoghurt and stevia into a bowl. Whisk together for a minute or so until well combined and a little frothy.

2. Divide between two small serving bowls or ramekins, then sprinkle an extra teaspoon of desiccated coconut over each serving and place in the fridge to set for at least an hour (overnight is ideal).

3. Serve with a dollop of coconut yoghurt and some fresh raspberries on top.

Mixed Berry Breakfast Parfait

Serves 2

2 x 170 g tubs plain fat-free Greek-style yoghurt

1 teaspoon vanilla extract

2 x 125 g punnets fresh berries of your choice (blueberries, raspberries, strawberries, blackberries)

1 small banana, sliced

Honey, for drizzling

Nut butter of your choice

45 g (½ cup) natural muesli (see recipe introduction)

Nothing beats the colourful layers of a berry parfait. This is a beautiful dish to enjoy when you're after a light breakfast or a more substantial snack. I've used natural muesli here, which is muesli that hasn't been toasted – this means it won't have had any oils or sweeteners, like maple syrup and honey, added to it. Natural muesli should only have a few very simple ingredients listed – things like rolled oats, nuts, seeds and plain dried fruits.

1. Mix the yoghurt and the vanilla extract together in a small bowl.
2. Using two good-sized glass tumblers, start to layer the parfait ingredients. First, divide half of the berries between the two glasses, then top with half of the yoghurt.
3. Arrange some banana slices on top, followed by a drizzle of honey and/or a dollop of nut butter. Divide most of the muesli between the two glasses, saving some for the top.
4. Repeat the layers with the remaining ingredients and finish with a sprinkle of muesli.

Chewy Banana and Oat Breakfast Cookies

Makes 6

1 small banana, mashed

45 g (½ cup) rolled oats

1 tablespoon desiccated coconut

1 teaspoon olive oil

1 teaspoon honey

½ teaspoon ground cinnamon

½ teaspoon vanilla extract

2 tablespoons sultanas or dark chocolate chips

I started making these cookies for my baby because they were so easy to whip together with one hand, and they had no added nasties. Needless to say the whole family enjoys them now. There is always a batch of these in our fridge.

1. Preheat the oven to 170°C. Line a baking tray with baking paper.

2. Place all of the ingredients except the sultanas/chocolate chips into a food processor and pulse until the mixture forms a chunky dough. Stir through the sultanas or chocolate chips.

3. Place heaped tablespoons of the dough onto the prepared tray, pressing down lightly on each with the back of the spoon to make a flat, round cookie shape. Don't worry about spacing the cookies too far apart – they won't spread when baking the way other cookies do.

4. Bake for about 20–25 minutes, or until the cookies are golden. Take the cookies out of the oven and leave them on the tray to cool for 5 minutes before transferring to a wire rack to cool completely.

Baked Peach
Crumble

Serves 2

2 large peaches

35 g (⅓ cup) rolled oats

1 tablespoon almond meal

1 tablespoon desiccated coconut

1 teaspoon coconut oil

1 teaspoon honey

½ teaspoon ground cinnamon

Sea salt

Ground nutmeg, for dusting over the top (optional)

plain Greek-style yoghurt, to serve

To enjoy this delicious crumble year-round, you can swap the peaches for small apples or pears – just core and cook for 10 to 15 minutes longer than the peaches, or until the fruit is soft.

1. Preheat the oven to 180°C.

2. Carefully run a small knife around the circumference of each peach. Gently twist each half away from the other to separate them. Pop out the stones and discard them.

3. Put the oats, almond meal, desiccated coconut, coconut oil, honey, cinnamon and a pinch of salt in a small bowl. Rub the ingredients together with your fingertips until everything is well combined and the mixture resembles biscuit crumbs.

4. Lay the peach halves, cut-side up, on a baking tray and pile the crumble mixture into the holes. Lightly dust the top of each one with nutmeg, if using.

5. Bake for around 30 minutes, or until the peaches are soft. If the crumble topping isn't golden enough for your liking, you can switch the oven to grill mode and brown it under the hot grill for a few minutes.

6. Serve two peach halves per person with a tablespoon or two of yoghurt.

5:2 option

Use olive oil spray instead of regular olive oil and omit the avocado.

| PER SERVE | *280* CALORIES | *1170* KILOJOULES |

Mexican Black Bean and Corn Frittata

Serves 2

4 eggs

2 tablespoons milk

½ teaspoon smoked paprika

Sea salt and freshly ground black pepper

½ tablespoon olive oil

1 spring onion, finely sliced

1 zucchini, quartered lengthways and diced

60 g (½ cup) finely diced red capsicum

100 g (½ cup) corn kernels

85 g (½ cup) drained and rinsed tinned black beans

1 tablespoon freshly grated parmesan

½ small avocado, peeled and sliced

When I first made this frittata, it was so substantial I could hardly believe it was a fasting meal. It's so wholesome and tasty and keeps me quite satisfied for many hours. I love it so much that it's become part of our regular routine, whether we're fasting or not. On a non-fast day I'll grate over some extra cheese and add some avocado, like I've done here. You can use fresh or tinned corn kernels for this.

1. Crack the eggs into a medium bowl and add the milk and paprika, and a pinch of salt and pepper. Whisk together well.

2. Preheat the oven grill to high.

3. Heat a medium (17 cm) non-stick frying pan over a medium–high heat and add the olive oil. Gently fry the spring onion, zucchini and red capsicum for 4–5 minutes, or until the veggies begin to soften.

4. To avoid a soggy frittata, pat the corn kernels and black beans dry with paper towel or a clean tea towel before adding them to the pan. Fry for 10–20 seconds.

5. Pour the egg mixture into the pan and use a spatula to move everything around so it doesn't catch on the bottom and the ingredients are evenly distributed. Sprinkle the grated parmesan over the top. Cook for 1–2 minutes, or until the outside of the frittata starts to set and become golden.

6. Place the pan under the oven grill for a minute or two, or until the top is golden and the frittata has set and is not wobbly.

7. Slice the frittata into quarters and serve two pieces per person with some sliced avocado on top.

Japanese Cabbage Omelette

Serves 2

50 g fresh thin egg noodles

4 eggs

1 tablespoon tamari or soy sauce

1 tablespoon olive oil

1 rasher short cut lean bacon, fat removed and finely sliced

2 spring onions, finely sliced

150 g (2 cups) finely shredded savoy or white cabbage

1 zucchini, coarsely grated

Sea salt and freshly ground black pepper

Dried chilli flakes or finely sliced fresh chilli, to serve (optional)

Kecap manis, to serve, optional

In Japan, this omelette is traditionally made more like a savoury pancake. My version has similar flavours, but without the pancake batter. Cabbage is a lovely addition – it bulks the dish out with tummy-filling fibre.

1. Place the egg noodles into a heatproof bowl and cover them with boiling water. Leave them for 5 minutes, then drain well – pat dry with paper towel, if needed – and set aside.

2. Crack the eggs into a medium bowl and add the tamari. Whisk together well, then set aside.

3. Heat a small non-stick frying pan over medium–high heat and add half of the olive oil. Add the bacon, half of the spring onion and all of the cabbage and zucchini. Add some freshly ground black pepper and a pinch of salt (the salt will help to draw out the liquid in the vegetables).

4. Fry gently until the vegetables are soft and the cabbage has wilted right down. The mixture should be fairly dry – this might take a few minutes. Spoon the cabbage mixture onto a plate and set aside.

5. Carefully wipe the pan out with paper towel and place it back on the heat. Add the remaining olive oil then pour in half the egg mixture. Cook for 1–2 minutes until it's starting to set around the edges and on top. Spoon half the cabbage mixture and half the egg noodles onto one side of the omelette, then gently fold the other half of the omelette over the filling.

6. Cook for another 20 seconds or so, then carefully flip the omelette over to cook the other side, if needed.

7. Transfer to a plate and serve topped with a pinch of fresh spring onion, a sprinkle of chilli flakes and a drizzle of kecap manis, if you like. Repeat with the remaining mixture to make the second omelette.

5:2 option

Use olive oil spray instead of regular olive oil. Omit the egg noodles and the kecap manis.

PER SERVE	200 CALORIES	836 KILOJOULES

Smoked Salmon Anytime Wrap

Serves 2

2 Mountain Bread wraps

2 tablespoons light cream cheese

100 g smoked salmon

½ avocado, peeled and sliced

50 g alfalfa sprouts

50 g baby spinach leaves

This recipe is so speedy and satisfying. It can be enjoyed for breakfast, lunch or dinner on a busy day.

1. Place a wrap on each plate.

2. Smear a tablespoon of cream cheese down the centre of each wrap and then divide the smoked salmon, avocado slices, alfalfa sprouts and baby spinach evenly between the two wraps.

3. Wrap tightly and enjoy!

Turmeric Scrambled Tofu and Peas

Serves 2

75 g (½ cup) frozen green peas

300 g firm tofu, drained and patted dry with paper towel

½ tablespoon olive oil

1 spring onion, finely sliced

½ teaspoon ground turmeric

A pinch of sea salt

2 tablespoons roughly chopped coriander (you could also use flat-leaf parsley)

2 slices of rye sourdough

Hummus (optional), to serve

Tofu is such a versatile and nutritious food – all it requires is some attentive flavouring and a little cooking and you have yourself a wonderful meal.

1. Blanch the peas for a few minutes and then drain well. Pat dry with paper towel and set aside.
2. Put the tofu in a medium bowl and use your hands to break it up, then use a masher to mash it until it resembles scrambled egg.
3. Heat a medium frying pan over medium–high heat and add the olive oil. Add the spring onion and fry for 30 seconds to soften, then add the tofu and fry for around 4 minutes. The tofu should release its liquid, so keep cooking until the liquid evaporates and it starts to fry.
4. Add the peas, turmeric, salt and coriander. Stir well, then turn off the heat.
5. Divide the tofu scramble between two bowls and serve with a slice of rye sourdough and a dollop of hummus, if you like.

Smashed Avo on Toast with Feta and Chilli

Serves 2

1 small avocado, peeled

Juice of 1 lime

Sea salt and freshly ground black pepper

1 large tomato, finely diced

1 spring onion, finely sliced

4 slices wholegrain bread, toasted

Chilli flakes (optional)

40 g goat's feta, to serve

Extra-virgin olive oil, to serve

Everyone's favourite brekkie of choice at the moment seems to be smashed avo on toast. You don't need to avoid it while you're fasting – it just needs a few minor tweaks to keep the calories low for a full fasting day.

1. Place the avocado in a small bowl, add the lime juice and a good pinch of salt and pepper. Mash everything together roughly with the back of a fork. Stir through the tomato and spring onion.

2. Top each slice of toast with the smashed avo. Sprinkle over a pinch of chilli, if you like, and some crumbled feta. Serve 2 slices of toast per person drizzled with some extra-virgin olive oil.

meat and
chicken

Chicken San Choy Bau

Serves 2

50 g vermicelli noodles

1 tablespoon olive oil

200 g chicken mince

2 spring onions, finely sliced

1 tablespoon minced ginger

2 garlic cloves, minced

150 g (about 1 bunch) bok choy, ends trimmed and chopped into 3 cm pieces, stems finely sliced

60 g (1 cup) broccoli, broken into small florets

65 g (½ cup) drained tinned bamboo shoots

1 x 230 g tin water chestnuts, drained and finely sliced

2 tablespoons tamari or soy sauce

Juice of ½ lime

1 teaspoon fish sauce

100 g (1 cup loosely packed) bean sprouts

2 tablespoons roughly chopped coriander or basil leaves

8 large iceberg or cos lettuce leaves, washed and patted dry

Finely sliced fresh chilli or dried chilli flakes (optional)

This is one of my favourite weekday meals! It's so flavoursome and filling, and the whole family enjoys it as well. There is something fun and exciting about filling the lettuce cups to make your own little wraps.

1. Cook the vermicelli noodles according to their packet instructions, then drain well and set aside.

2. Heat a large wok or heavy-based frying pan over a medium–high heat. Add the olive oil and the chicken mince. Break the mince up with a spoon or a spatula as you move it around the wok. Fry for a few minutes until it starts to colour and is cooked through.

3. Add the spring onion, ginger and garlic to the chicken and stir well. Then add the bok choy, broccoli, bamboo shoots and water chestnuts, and continue to stir-fry for a few more minutes until the vegetables soften.

4. In a small bowl, combine the tamari, lime juice and fish sauce and whisk with a fork. Pour this over the chicken mixture and stir together well before tossing in the noodles.

5. Turn the heat off, add the bean sprouts and coriander and mix through.

6. To serve, place spoonfuls of the chicken mixture into each lettuce cup. Top with a sprinkle of fresh or dried chilli, if you wish.

5:2 option

Omit the vermicelli
noodles.

| PER SERVE | 195 CALORIES | 815 KILOJOULES |

Bunless Lamb and Mushroom Burger

Serves 2

200 g extra lean lamb mince

1 teaspoon finely chopped rosemary or dried rosemary

Sea salt and freshly ground black pepper

1 large sweet potato, halved and sliced into thin wedges

Olive oil spray

1 large onion, finely sliced

4 large field mushrooms (equivalent in size to a burger bun), peeled and stalks removed

4 large lettuce leaves

2 tablespoons tomato sauce (go for a brand with no added sugar)

½ carrot, coarsely grated

1 large tomato, finely sliced

2 teaspoons Dijon mustard (or mustard of your choice)

2 large gherkins (look for an unsweetened variety, like polskie ogorki), halved

Burgers get such a bad rap for being unhealthy, but if you use good-quality lean mince, extra salad fillings and low-calorie sauces, a burger can be a beautifully balanced meal.

1. Preheat the oven to 190°C.

2. Place the lamb and the rosemary in a large bowl and season with salt and pepper. Mix together with clean hands until well combined. Then, with damp hands, divide the mixture in half and roll each half into a ball. Gently flatten each ball with your hand until it's about 2–3 cm thick, then place on a plate in the fridge for 20 minutes or so to firm up. Take the burger patties out of the fridge 5–10 minutes before cooking.

3. Place the sweet potato wedges in a small roasting dish then spray lightly with olive oil and season generously with salt and pepper. Toss to coat and then bake in the oven for 30 minutes, or until crispy and golden.

4. Heat a griddle pan, large frying pan or a barbecue hotplate over a medium heat. Spray with olive oil, then add the onion and sprinkle over a pinch of salt. Cook slowly, stirring occasionally until the onion is soft. Move the fried onion to a small plate and add the four mushrooms to the pan. Cook them on each side for a few minutes, until soft but still holding their shape well. Remove from the pan and set aside.

5. Wipe the pan out with paper towel and turn the heat up to high. Spray the pan with olive oil again before adding the lamb patties. Cook for a few minutes on each side for medium–well done. Once cooked to your liking, transfer to a plate to rest for a minute or two. If you haven't already done so, take the sweet potato wedges out of the oven and let cool for a minute.

6. Construct each burger starting with a mushroom, stem-side up, then a lettuce leaf, lamb patty, tomato sauce, some onion, slices of tomato and grated carrot. Smear the inside of the second mushroom with a teaspoon of mustard and place it on top.

7. Serve each burger with a sliced gherkin on the side and some sweet potato wedges.

'Sort of' Spaghetti and Turkey Meatballs

Serves 2

250 g turkey breast mince

½ teaspoon dried oregano

1 tablespoon finely chopped flat-leaf parsley

Sea salt and freshly ground black pepper

1 tablespoon olive oil

½ onion, finely diced

1 garlic clove, minced

1 x 400 g tin chopped tomatoes

2 tablespoons red wine

2 teaspoons Worcestershire sauce

1 tablespoon tomato paste

1 teaspoon stock powder or 1 stock cube (chicken or vegetable)

250 g egg noodles

2 tablespoons freshly grated parmesan

The ultimate comfort food is spaghetti and meatballs but it can be very high in calories. This version has a few clever adjustments that reduce the calories while also giving it a nutritional boost.

1. In a medium bowl, combine the turkey mince, oregano, parsley and a good pinch of salt and pepper. Mix together well with clean hands, then with damp hands, roll the turkey mixture into 2–3 cm balls (you should get around 10 of them). Place these on a plate, then cover and refrigerate for at least 20 minutes.

2. Heat a heavy-based saucepan over medium heat. Add the olive oil and the onion and a pinch of salt. Fry gently for 5 minutes, or until the onion becomes translucent and golden. Add the garlic and the tinned tomatoes. Fill the empty tomato tin with water and add that to the pan too.

3. Add the red wine to the pan with the Worcestershire sauce, tomato paste, stock and a good grind of pepper and give it a good stir. Bring to the boil, then reduce the heat and simmer uncovered for about 10 minutes, or until the sauce has reduced slightly and is beginning to thicken.

4. Place the meatballs into the sauce and give the pan a bit of a shake to distribute them evenly. Put the lid on and allow to simmer for 10–15 minutes, giving the pan a gentle shake or a stir occasionally.

5. In the meantime, cook the egg noodles according to the packet instructions. Once cooked, distribute between two bowls.

6. Top each bowl of noodles with half of the meatballs, and sprinkle a tablespoon of grated parmesan over each portion before serving.

Chunky Chicken and Vegetable Soup

Serves 6

1 tablespoon olive oil, plus extra for drizzling

1 leek, white and light green parts only, washed and finely sliced

1 large carrot, roughly diced

4 celery stalks, roughly chopped

Sea salt and freshly ground black pepper

4 skinless chicken thigh fillets

1 tablespoon chicken stock powder

1 zucchini, roughly diced

¼ head cauliflower, broken into small florets

70 g (2 cups) roughly chopped silverbeet

4 heaped tablespoons roughly chopped flat-leaf parsley

A slice of sourdough per person, toasted

Whether I'm fasting or not, this recipe is on high rotation in our house, particularly in winter. It's a great way to minimise waste because it provides the perfect excuse to use up any sad-looking vegetables in the fridge, plus it's a tasty way of getting in your daily dose of vegetables!

1. Heat a stockpot or a large saucepan over medium–high heat. Add the olive oil, leek, carrot, celery and a good pinch of salt and pepper, and fry gently for at least 5 minutes to allow the vegetables to soften and partially cook.
2. Add 1.2 litres of water to the pot and turn the heat up to high. Add the chicken thighs and stock powder and bring to the boil, then immediately turn the heat down to medium–low. Place a lid on the pot and continue to simmer for at least 1½ hours, or until the chicken is cooked through and the vegetables are tender.
3. Once cooked, you can stir the soup with a fork and the chicken should easily shred apart. If you prefer, you can use tongs to remove each chicken thigh to a board so you can shred the meat with a fork and then return it to the soup.
4. Turn the heat back up to medium and add the zucchini, cauliflower and silverbeet. Cook for 10 minutes.
5. Once the soup is ready, turn off the heat and stir through most of the parsley. Serve each portion of soup topped with a pinch of fresh parsley and a toasted slice of sourdough drizzled with a little olive oil.

Mexican Turkey Stuffed Capsicums

Serves 2

1 tablespoon olive oil

200 g turkey breast mince

2 spring onions, finely sliced

1 teaspoon minced garlic

1 x 400 g tin crushed tomatoes

65 g (⅓ cup) drained and rinsed tinned red kidney or black beans

65 g (⅓ cup) corn kernels

1 celery stalk, finely diced

½ carrot, finely diced

½ large zucchini, finely diced

½ teaspoon smoked paprika

½ teaspoon ground cumin

½ teaspoon dried oregano

Freshly ground black pepper

½ teaspoon chilli powder (optional)

½ teaspoon chicken stock powder

185 g (1 cup) cooked quinoa

2 tablespoons roughly sliced coriander leaves + extra sprigs to serve

2 large red capsicums, halved lengthways and deseeded

Grated cheddar

Stuffed capsicums usually call for a combination of rice and mince, but this recipe just uses lean mince and is packed with vegetables and delicious spices, which makes it a great option if you need to tweak it for a lower-calorie fasting day.

1. Preheat the oven to 180°C.

2. Heat a large non-stick frying pan over medium–high heat and add the olive oil. Add the turkey mince and fry until browned and cooked through, breaking the mince up with a spatula or spoon as it cooks.

3. Add the spring onion, garlic, tomatoes, beans, corn, celery, carrot, zucchini, paprika, cumin, oregano and a good grind of pepper. Add the chilli powder, too, if you're using it. Stir everything together well.

4. Dissolve the stock powder in 250 ml (1 cup) boiling water and add to the frying pan. Bring everything to the boil, then reduce the heat and simmer for around 10–15 minutes, or until most of the liquid has evaporated and you have a reasonably dry mixture. Turn off the heat and stir through the quinoa and the coriander.

5. Tuck the capsicum halves, cut-side up, snugly into a baking dish. Fill each capsicum half with a quarter of the turkey mixture. Cover the dish tightly with foil and bake for around 35 minutes, then remove the foil, sprinkle liberally with the cheddar and return to the oven until the capsicums are soft and tender and the cheese has melted.

6. Serve two capsicum halves per person, with the extra coriander leaves sprinkled on top.

5:2 option

Omit the rice. Because there won't be any rice to hold the ingredients in, it's best to fold in the shorter side of the nori roll first, about 1 cm or so, then start from the bottom and roll the rest of the sushi tightly.

CALORIES PER SERVE (3 ROLLS)

260	1087
CALORIES	KILOJOULES

DIY Chicken Teriyaki Hand Rolls

Serves 2

RICE

200 g (1 cup) short-grain brown rice, rinsed and drained

2 teaspoons rice wine vinegar

Sea salt

FILLING

200 g chicken breast (or tempeh, for a vegan option)

2 tablespoons teriyaki sauce

Olive oil spray

6 nori sheets

70 g (1 cup) finely sliced red cabbage

70 g (1 cup) finely sliced white cabbage

1 Lebanese cucumber, finely sliced into matchsticks

1 carrot, finely sliced into matchsticks

½ small avocado, peeled and thinly sliced

1 tablespoon pickled ginger (optional)

Tamari or soy sauce, to serve

Wasabi, to serve

Japanese hand rolls make for a light and nourishing meal, and they are easily adapted for a fasting day. These rolls are packed with lots of colourful raw vegetables and pickled ginger, then wrapped in seaweed.

1. Cook the rice according to the packet instructions. Once cooked, turn the heat off but keep the lid on and allow to cool for at least 10 minutes. Add the rice wine vinegar and a pinch of salt and stir through – the rice should be slightly sticky.

2. Place the chicken on a large piece of baking paper and fold the paper over so the chicken is completely covered on both sides. Use a rolling pin or meat mallet to pound the chicken until it is about 1 cm thick all over. Place it in a small bowl and cover with the teriyaki sauce, then place in the fridge to marinate for at least 30 minutes.

3. Heat a non-stick frying pan over medium–high heat and spray with olive oil. Add the chicken to the hot pan and cook for 2–3 minutes on each side, or until golden and cooked through (the thinner the piece of chicken, the faster it will cook). Once cooked, take the chicken off the heat and allow it to rest for 5 minutes before slicing thinly.

4. To construct each sushi roll, place a nori sheet shiny-side down on your work surface (or use a bamboo mat if you have one). Spread a thin layer of rice over half the sheet. Place a pinch of red cabbage horizontally down the centre of the nori sheet, followed by a pinch of white cabbage. On top of that, place a few sticks of cucumber, carrot, avocado and then a couple of chicken slices. Add a few pieces of pickled ginger, if you wish. Repeat to make 6 rolls in total.

5. Serve 3 rolls per person, with tamari or soy sauce for dipping and some wasabi, if you like.

Capricciosa Pizzas

Serves 2 (2 pizzas per person)

4 small wholemeal pita pockets (about 70 g each)

4 tablespoons tomato paste

100 g lean ham off the bone (omit for a vegetarian option)

8 button mushrooms, finely sliced

8 marinated artichoke hearts, roughly chopped

16 pitted black olives, sliced

Shredded light mozzarella

A handful of fresh basil leaves, torn

I've heard it said that there's no such thing as bad pizza and I agree! I also think pizza should be enjoyed any time, including when you're fasting. This lighter version has the look and feel of a pizza but without the heavier calories from a doughy base and overly cheesy topping.

1. Preheat the oven to 200°C.
2. Line a baking tray with baking paper and put the pitas on the tray. Dollop half the tomato paste in the middle of each pita pocket and spread it around using the back of a spoon.
3. Top each pizza with ham, mushroom and artichoke. Scatter the olives and the shredded mozzarella over the pizzas.
4. Bake in the hot oven for 15–20 minutes, or until golden and melty, then serve with the torn basil leaves scattered over.

Beef Pho

Serves 2

½ tablespoon olive oil

½ white onion, thinly sliced

Sea salt

500 ml (2 cups) beef bone broth (or good quality beef stock)

1 slice ginger, about 5 mm thick

1 garlic clove, finely sliced

2 star anise

1 cinnamon stick

1 tablespoon fish sauce

50 g dried flat rice noodles

100 g beef eye fillet, sliced very thinly, about 2–3 mm (see recipe introduction)

100 g (1 cup) bean sprouts

2 small handfuls of coriander leaves

2 small handfuls of Thai basil leaves (or regular basil, if you can't find Thai basil)

2 small handfuls mint leaves

1 lime, halved

Long red chilli, finely sliced, to serve (optional)

Pho is a traditional Vietnamese soup with a rich broth and a thick noodle base. You can add beef, chicken or seafood to make a filling and flavourful soup. A great tip I've learned is to freeze the beef fillet the night before, to make it easier to cut into very thin slices. Once sliced, allow the meat to thaw for 5 to 10 minutes before adding it to the hot broth.

1. Place a medium-sized saucepan over medium heat and add the olive oil. Add the onion and a pinch of salt and fry for a couple of minutes until soft.

2. Add the broth, ginger, garlic, star anise, cinnamon and fish sauce to the pan. Turn the heat up to high and bring to the boil. Once boiling, turn the heat down, cover with a lid and simmer for 15–20 minutes.

3. In the meantime, prepare the noodles according to the packet instructions, then drain and set aside.

4. Use a slotted spoon to remove the solid ingredients from the broth; discard these.

5. To serve, divide the noodles between two bowls, then top with slices of beef and ladle over the hot broth – the beef will be cooked by the heat of the broth.

6. Top with bean sprouts and herbs, then squeeze a lime half over each bowl. Sprinkle over chilli, as you wish.

5:2 option

Use olive oil spray instead of regular olive oil. Use a 400 g packet of Slendier Noodles in place of the flat rice noodles.

| PER SERVE | 110 CALORIES | 460 KILOJOULES |

Honey Soy Pork Tenderloin

Serves 2

1 x 300 g lean pork fillet, fat trimmed

1 tablespoon sesame seeds

200 g (1 cup) brown rice

200 g green beans, trimmed

HONEY SOY MARINADE

1 tablespoon honey

125 ml (½ cup) tamari or soy sauce

2 teaspoons minced garlic

2 teaspoons minced ginger

1 teaspoon olive oil

This sweet and sticky dish is so satisfying! Pork is an excellent source of lean protein and, in fact, it's lighter in calories than both chicken and turkey breast.

1. Pat the pork fillet dry with paper towel then place in a large ziplock bag.

2. Mix all of the marinade ingredients together in a small bowl, then pour into the bag with the pork fillet. Seal the bag and move the fillet around inside the bag so the marinade completely covers the pork. Place in the fridge and leave to marinate for at least an hour.

3. Preheat the oven to 170°C. Line a baking tray with baking paper.

4. Place the marinated pork on the prepared tray. Sprinkle over the sesame seeds and bake for 25–30 minutes, or until cooked to your liking.

5. Meanwhile, cook the brown rice according to the packet instructions.

6. Once out of the oven, allow the pork to rest for 5 minutes. Steam the green beans.

7. Slice the pork, then divide the slices between two plates and serve with the green beans and brown rice.

Korean Beef Bibimbap

Serves 2

1 tablespoon olive oil

200 g extra-lean beef mince

1 spring onion, finely sliced

½ teaspoon minced garlic

1 tablespoon tamari or soy sauce

200 g (1 cup) white or brown rice

100 g baby spinach leaves

Sea salt

1 teaspoon sesame oil

2 teaspoons toasted sesame seeds

150 g (1½ cups) bean sprouts

2 eggs

1 carrot, cut finely into matchsticks

2 heaped tablespoons kimchi

Chilli sauce (optional), to serve

This Korean dish is a dietitian's dream because it's nutrionally balanced. There's lean protein, plenty of veg and some carbs, plus the added bonus of tummy-friendly fermented kimchi.

1. Start by preparing the beef mince. Heat a large non-stick frying pan over medium–high heat. Add half of the olive oil and all of the mince, breaking up the mince with a spatula or spoon as it cooks.

2. Add the spring onion, garlic and tamari, and continue to fry for another minute until the mince has browned. Set aside on a plate.

3. Cook the rice according to the packet instructions, then set aside while you bring the other elements together.

4. Bring a small saucepan of water to the boil. Add the baby spinach to the boiling water for 30 seconds or so, then remove with a slotted spoon into a colander to drain. When cool, use your hands to squeeze out the excess water, then place the spinach on a clean tea towel or paper towel to dry completely. Once dry, add the spinach to a medium bowl, season with salt, then sprinkle with the sesame oil and seeds and toss together.

5. Meanwhile, add the bean sprouts to the boiling water for 30 seconds, then drain and pat dry with paper towel.

6. Wipe the frying pan out with paper towel, then return it to the heat. Add the remaining olive oil, crack in the eggs and cook them to your liking – sunny-side up or over-easy for a well-cooked yolk. Set the cooked eggs aside on a plate.

7. Construct the bibimbap by dividing the rice between two bowls. Place half of each of the remaining ingredients in small mounds around the bowl, on top of the rice – the beef mince, spinach, sprouts, carrot and kimchi. Top each with a fried egg and then douse with chilli sauce, if you wish.

seafood

Prawn
Pad Thai

Serves 2

½ x 250 g packet dried thick
rice noodles

2 tablespoons tamari or soy sauce

1 tablespoon natural peanut butter

1 tablespoon olive oil

200 g uncooked prawns, shelled
and deveined

1 garlic clove, minced or finely diced

1 teaspoon minced or finely
diced ginger

2 spring onions, finely sliced

1 bunch bok choy or choy sum,
roughly chopped

60 g (½ cup) finely sliced
red capsicum

20 snow peas, halved

Finely sliced fresh chilli, dried chilli
flakes or Sriracha sauce (optional)

100 g (1 cup) bean sprouts

2 tablespoons roughly
chopped coriander

2 tablespoons roughly chopped
roasted peanuts or cashews

**The traditional version of this dish can come in at around
a thousand calories per serve and contain the equivalent
carbohydrates to half a loaf of bread! My version is bulked
out with vegetables to keep it lighter, and if you want
a fasting version, you can make it even less calorific by
using carbohydrate-free konjac noodles.**

1. Cook the noodles according to the packet instructions,
then drain and lay out on a clean tea towel to dry completely
(this is really important!).
2. In a small bowl, whisk the tamari and peanut butter together.
3. Heat a wok or a non-stick frying pan over medium–high
heat. Add half of the olive oil to the pan and then the prawns.
Stir-fry, tossing constantly, until the prawns are no longer
translucent; this should only take a minute or two. Place them
in a bowl and set aside.
4. Add the remaining olive oil to the wok, return it to the heat
and add the garlic, ginger, spring onion, bok choy, capsicum
and snow peas. Stir-fry for a few minutes, moving everything
around regularly, until the vegetables begin to soften.
5. Add the noodles and prawns to the wok and toss everything
together well. Pour over the peanut sauce and add some
chilli, if you like. Stir-fry for another couple of minutes, until
everything is well combined.
6. Divide between two bowls and serve topped with the bean
sprouts, coriander and some roasted peanuts or cashews
sprinkled on top.

Salmon and Pumpkin Fish Burgers

Serves 2

1 salmon fillet (125 g), skin and bones removed, roughly chopped

1 egg

75 g (½ cup) diced Kent pumpkin, cooked and mashed

50 g dried breadcrumbs

1 tablespoon finely chopped flat-leaf parsley

Sea salt and freshly ground black pepper

Olive oil spray

2 hamburger buns or soft rolls (preferably wholegrain)

Tartare sauce, to serve

Cos lettuce, to serve

This recipe came about when I was trying to come up with nutritious and quick meals for my baby. The patties were so yummy that the rest of the family got into them too, especially when I used them for fish burgers. The simple ingredients in the patties make them nutritious, but also great for a low-calorie fasting day meal.

1. Preheat the oven to 180°C. Line a baking tray with baking paper.
2. Place the salmon, egg, pumpkin, breadcrumbs and parsley into a food processor and season with salt and pepper. Pulse until combined – the mixture should be a chunky puree.
3. Using slightly damp hands, divide the mixture in half, then spoon onto the baking tray and form 2 x 2 cm-thick patties.
4. Lightly spray the patties with olive oil, then place in the oven for 15 minutes, or until golden and cooked through.
5. Place some cos lettuce on each bun base, top with a fishcake and a teaspoon of tartare sauce, then add the bun lids and serve.

Tandoori Fish with Cumin-spiced Basmati Rice

Serves 2

2 firm white fish fillets (200 g), such as ling, skin and bones removed

½ tablespoon tandoori paste

2 tablespoons plain fat-free Greek-style yoghurt

100 g (½ cup) basmati rice

½ teaspoon ground cumin

1 lemon, halved

2 spring onions, finely sliced

Sea salt and freshly ground black pepper

2 tablespoons roughly chopped coriander

Indian food is rich in flavour but is often rich in calories too, thanks to the coconut cream and ghee used in many dishes. This lovely, light dish has all the flavour of your favourite Indian meal without the extra fat and calories.

1. Preheat the oven to 180°C. Line a baking tray with baking paper and place the fish fillets on the tray.

2. In a small bowl, mix together the tandoori paste and the yoghurt. Divide the mixture between the two fish fillets and use the back of a spoon to spread it evenly all over each fillet. Bake the fish for 15 minutes, or until cooked through and golden on top.

3. While the fish is cooking, prepare the rice. Add the cumin, juice of ½ a lemon, the spring onion and a good pinch of salt and pepper to the rice before cooking according to the packet instructions.

4. Divide the cooked rice between two plates, then top with a tandoori fish fillet and sprinkle over the coriander leaves. Serve with wedges of lemon for squeezing over.

How to make cumin-spiced broccoli and cauliflower 'rice' (great for fasting days!)

Break ½ a head of broccoli and ¼ a head of cauliflower into florets. Pulse in a food processor until they resemble rice, then heat a large frying pan over medium heat and spray with olive oil. Add the spring onion and fry gently for a minute, then add the 'rice' and continue to fry for 2 minutes. Sprinkle over the cumin and a good pinch of salt and pepper. Squeeze over the juice of ½ a lemon. Fry for 2–3 minutes or until soft and just starting to turn golden, then serve.

Prawn Tom Yum Soup

Serves 2

1 tablespoon tom yum paste

500 ml (2 cups) chicken or fish stock (buy liquid stock or make it up using stock powder and boiling water)

1 teaspoon coconut sugar

2 teaspoons fish sauce

120 g (1 cup) button mushrooms, trimmed

10 cherry tomatoes, halved

100 g green beans, trimmed and halved

150 g (1 bunch) bok choy, roughly diced

250 g uncooked prawns, shelled and deveined

50 g thick rice noodles

Juice of ½ lime

2 heaped tablespoons roughly chopped coriander

Traditionally, there are two styles of tom yum soup; one is a creamy soup that uses evaporated milk in the base, the other is a sweet and sour soup with a clear broth. The second version is my preferred go-to because it's a little lighter.

1. Place the tom yum paste and the stock in a large saucepan and bring to a simmer over a medium heat. Stir in the coconut sugar and fish sauce.

2. Add the mushrooms, cherry tomatoes, green beans and bok choy and simmer for 5 more minutes, or until the vegetables have softened.

3. Add the prawns and rice noodles and cook for another 2–3 minutes, or until the prawns are cooked through and no longer translucent.

4. Turn off the heat and stir in the lime juice and coriander. Divide between two bowls and serve right away.

5:2 option

Omit the rice noodles.

PER SERVE	123 CALORIES	514 KILOJOULES

Creamy Tuna Salad

Serves 2

TUNA MIXTURE

1 x 180 g tin good-quality tuna in oil, drained

2 teaspoons whole egg mayo

2 heaped tablespoons cottage cheese

Juice of 1 lemon

Sea salt and freshly ground black pepper

1 x 125 g tin corn kernels, drained

1 tablespoon roughly chopped flat-leaf parsley (or other soft herb of your choice)

SALAD BASE

4 cups mixed vegetables (I like a combination of the following: lettuce, spinach, rocket, grated carrot, shredded red or white cabbage, finely sliced fennel, diced celery and sliced cucumber)

TO SERVE

1 small avocado, peeled and roughly diced

Good crusty grain bread, for serving

A tuna salad is a lunch favourite but what makes it yummy for me is adding a delicious creamy dressing – unfortunately, this tends to add a lot of extra calories. My version tastes like a delicious ranch dressing and is a whole lot better for you, too!

1. In a large bowl, combine the tuna, mayonnaise, cottage cheese and half the lemon juice. Add a pinch of salt and a good grind of pepper and mash until mixed together. Stir through the corn and the parsley.

2. Add the tuna mixture to your salad base along with the remaining lemon juice. Toss together well.

3. Divide between two bowls and top with diced avocado. Serve immediately with a slice of bread.

5:2 option

Omit the avocado and
the bread.

PER SERVE	270 CALORIES	1129 KILOJOULES

Garlic Mixed Seafood Noodles

Serves 2

2 tablespoons olive oil + extra for serving

1 onion, finely sliced

Sea salt and freshly ground black pepper

100 g whole egg fettuccine

400 g marinara mix (see recipe introduction)

1 tablespoon minced garlic

Zest and juice of 1 lemon

2 tablespoons roughly chopped flat-leaf parsley + a little extra for serving

Mixed seafood (or marinara mix) is a mixture of diced fish, prawns, calamari and octopus that can be bought from some supermarkets or good fish shops. It's a really convenient ingredient, and a great source of protein when you're fasting because it's very light in calories and so versatile. This simple dish can be whipped up quickly and is perfect for a fast weekday dinner.

1. Heat a large heavy-based non-stick frying pan over medium heat and add 1 tablespoon of olive oil. Add the onion and a pinch of salt, then cook for about 2–3 minutes until the onion is soft. Set the onion aside in a large bowl.
2. Meanwhile, cook the fettuccine according to the packet instructions, then drain and set aside in a colander.
3. Place the frying pan over high heat and add ½ a tablespoon of olive oil to the pan. Add half of the marinara mixture, moving everything around the pan quickly. Fry until the seafood is no longer translucent and is starting to turn golden. Transfer the cooked seafood to the bowl with the onion, then place the pan back on the heat and repeat with the rest of the olive oil and the remaining seafood mixture (it's best to cook it in two batches to make sure the pan stays hot and the seafood cooks evenly).
4. Once the second batch of seafood is cooked, return the onion and first batch of seafood to the pan, then add the garlic, lemon zest, juice and parsley and give it all a good stir. Cook for a minute or two, then add the drained fettuccine to the pan and gently toss everything together.
5. Divide the seafood and noodles between two bowls and serve with a drizzle of olive oil and the extra parsley.

Italian Seafood Stew

Serves 2

SEAFOOD STEW

¼ teaspoon (a pinch) of saffron threads

1 tablespoon olive oil

1 onion, finely sliced

Sea salt and freshly ground black pepper

¼ large fennel bulb, finely sliced

1 celery stalk, finely sliced

1 carrot, halved and finely sliced

1 teaspoon minced garlic

1 teaspoon paprika

½ teaspoon dried thyme

3 tablespoons white wine

1 x 400 g tin chopped tomatoes

375 ml (1½ cups) fish or chicken stock

Juice of ½ lemon

250 g firm white fish, cut into 2 cm pieces

8 large cooked prawns, peeled

8 mussels, scrubbed clean and beards removed

2 heaped tablespoons roughly chopped flat-leaf parsley

Grated parmesan, to serve

PARMESAN TOAST

2 thick slices sourdough bread

Extra-virgin olive oil, for drizzling

2 tablespoons grated parmesan

My inspiration for this meal comes from my favourite local Italian restaurant. They do the richest, most flavoursome seafood stew – I crave it if I haven't had it for a while. There is a little wine in this recipe, but the alcohol will cook off so you end up with the flavour of wine, without the calories.

1. Place the saffron threads in a small bowl or mug with 1 tablespoon hot water. Set aside while you start the stew.
2. Heat a large, heavy-based saucepan over medium heat. Add the olive oil, onion and a pinch of salt. Fry gently for around 5 minutes, or until the onion is soft. Add the fennel, celery and carrot and continue to fry for another 5 minutes or so, until the other vegetables are starting to soften.
3. Add the minced garlic, paprika, thyme and a generous pinch of pepper and give it all a good stir. Add the wine, increase the heat to high and cook for 1 minute. Reduce the heat back down to medium, then add the tomatoes, stock, the saffron and its soaking water, and the lemon juice. Stir together well, then simmer uncovered for 10 minutes, or until the sauce has thickened slightly.
4. In the meantime, prepare the parmesan toast. Preheat the grill to medium–high. Drizzle each slice of sourdough on one side with olive oil and sprinkle a tablespoon of grated parmesan over each slice. Place under the grill and toast for 3–4 minutes, or until the edges of the toast and the parmesan are golden. You only want to toast one side.
5. Add the seafood to the pan, gently pushing it all down so it is completely submerged in the stew. Cover and allow to simmer over a low heat for 5 minutes, or until the seafood is cooked through and the mussels have all opened (discard any that don't open).
6. Divide the stew between two bowls, then top each serving with a tablespoon of parsley and a good grating of parmesan. Serve with the parmesan toast.

Quick Salmon with Mixed Veg Mash

Serves 2

2 x 125 g salmon fillets

Sea salt and freshly ground black pepper

1 tablespoon olive oil

75 g (½ cup) peeled and diced pumpkin

½ large carrot, diced

60 g (½ cup) broccoli florets

60 g (½ cup) cauliflower florets

1 tablespoon freshly grated parmesan

1 teaspoon butter

1 tablespoon milk

1 teaspoon roughly chopped flat-leaf parsley

½ lemon, cut into wedges

Salmon with mashed potato is a match made in foodie heaven, but potato mash can be high in calories and not terribly nutritious. My version uses four vegetable favourites, and it makes a delicious alternative to your standard mash.

1. Season each side of the salmon fillets with salt and pepper. Heat a non-stick frying pan over medium–high heat and add the olive oil to the pan. Fry the fish, skin-side down, for about 5–7 minutes or until crisp and golden, then flip and cook for another 5 minutes or until cooked to your liking.

2. While the salmon is cooking, put all of the vegetables in a steamer basket placed over a large saucepan over high heat. Steam until they are soft – a knife should be able to pass through the largest vegetables easily.

3. Empty the water from the saucepan, then put the vegetables into the warm pan and place it over a low heat. Add the parmesan, butter and milk and season well with salt and pepper. Mash until the vegetables are well mixed, but still have a chunky texture.

4. Spoon half of the mashed veggies into a mound on each of two plates, and place a salmon fillet on top of each mound. Serve straight away, with the parsley scattered on top and a wedge of lemon for squeezing over.

5:2 option

Omit the potatoes and the extra drizzle of olive oil.

PER SERVE	*265* CALORIES	*1108* KILOJOULES

Tuna Nicoise Salad

Serves 2

4 large cos or iceberg lettuce leaves, roughly chopped

½ small red onion, finely sliced

10 cherry tomatoes, halved

100 g green beans, ends trimmed, halved and blanched

10 kalamata olives

1 x 185 g tin tuna in olive oil, drained

2 hardboiled eggs, peeled and cut into eighths

6 new or chat potatoes, boiled and halved

DRESSING

1 teaspoon extra-virgin olive oil + extra, to serve

2 tablespoons lemon juice

½ teaspoon Dijon mustard

A pinch of sea salt and freshly ground black pepper

This classic French salad is always a winner. It's light but beautifully balanced, and all you need to do to enjoy it as a delicious, low-calorie meal on a full fasting day is omit the potato and the extra splash of oil.

1. Whisk the dressing ingredients together in a small bowl (or shake them together in a small jar to mix, if you prefer).
2. Divide the lettuce, onion, tomatoes, green beans and olives between two bowls or plates. Top with chunks of tuna, hardboiled egg and potatoes.
3. Drizzle the dressing over the top and add another splash of extra-virgin olive oil before serving, if you like.

Fish Tacos with Cabbage Salad

Serves 2

1 teaspoon olive oil

1 tablespoon lime juice

1 teaspoon minced garlic

½ teaspoon smoked paprika

½ teaspoon ground cumin

½ teaspoon chilli powder

Sea salt and freshly ground black pepper

2 firm white fish fillets (200 g), skin and bones removed

CABBAGE SALAD

70 g (1 cup) shredded red cabbage

70 g (1 cup) shredded white cabbage

½ carrot, grated

1 spring onion, finely chopped

2 tablespoons roughly chopped coriander

1 tablespoon lime juice

SAUCE

1 tablespoon plain fat-free Greek-style yoghurt

1 tablespoon no-added-sugar tomato sauce

Juice of ½ lime

Pinch of sea salt

A few drops of Tabasco sauce, to taste

GUACAMOLE

1 avocado

Juice of 1 lime

Sea salt

6–8 flour tortillas, heated on a griddle pan, to serve

There's something so satisfying about diving in and using your hands to construct and wrap these delicious parcels. My fish tacos are perfect for sharing and can be enjoyed by everyone, fasting or not!

1. In a large bowl, whisk together the olive oil, lime juice, garlic, paprika, cumin, chilli powder, salt and pepper. Add the fish and turn over in the marinade until well covered. Cover the bowl and place in the fridge for at least 20 minutes to marinate.

2. To make the cabbage salad, place all the ingredients in a bowl, season with salt and pepper and mix to combine.

3. To make the sauce, place all of the ingredients in a small bowl and mix together well.

4. To make the guacamole, place the avocado flesh into a small bowl and mash with the back of a fork until mostly smooth but still a bit chunky. Add the lime juice, season well with salt and stir together.

5. Heat a non-stick frying pan over high heat (you could also use the oven grill or a barbecue). Cook the fish fillets for a few minutes on each side until cooked through and golden on the outside. Rest the fillets on a plate for a minute or two before breaking up into large chunks.

6. Assemble the tacos by dividing the fish between the tortillas. Add some cabbage salad, a dollop of sauce and a spoonful of guacamole to each tortilla, then wrap up and enjoy!

vegetarian
meals

5:2 option

Use only olive oil spray instead of regular olive oil and swap the brown rice for broccoli and cauliflower 'rice' (half a head each; see page 150 for prep instructions). Allow to cool completely before adding in Step 3.

| PER SERVE | 250 CALORIES | 1045 KILOJOULES |

Nasi Goreng

Serves 2

200 g (1 cup) long grain brown rice

1 tablespoon olive oil

200 g firm tofu, cut into 2 cm cubes

1 tablespoon Sriracha sauce

½ onion, finely sliced

1 garlic clove, minced

1 teaspoon minced ginger

2 tablespoons tamari or soy sauce

10 cherry tomatoes, halved

100 g baby spinach leaves

100 g (1 cup) bean sprouts

A handful of coriander leaves, roughly chopped

1 lime, halved

Olive oil spray

2 eggs

1 spring onion, finely sliced

1 Lebanese cucumber, finely sliced

Fresh red chilli, finely sliced or dried chilli flakes, to serve (optional)

Nasi goreng is a traditional Indonesian dish with a rice base – a little like fried rice with an egg on top. I've packed this version full of vegetables for a nutritionally boosted meal. If you're after a low-calorie option, swapping out the rice for broccoli and cauliflower 'rice' is an easy fix.

1. Cook the rice according to the packet instructions, then drain well and spread out on a baking tray lined with a clean tea towel to cool completely while you prepare the rest of the ingredients.

2. Heat a large non-stick frying pan or a wok over medium-high heat with half of the olive oil. Add the tofu, top with the Sriracha chilli sauce and toss around for a minute or two, or until golden. Transfer to a plate and set aside.

3. Carefully wipe the pan out with paper towel then add the remaining olive oil and return to the heat. Add the onion and fry for 5 minutes, or until the onion is beginning to soften. Add the cooled rice and fry gently for 1–2 minutes.

4. Next, add the garlic, ginger and tamari and give everything a good mix. Then add the tomatoes, spinach leaves, bean sprouts and half of the coriander, then squeeze over the juice of half a lime and mix through. Stir occasionally until the spinach leaves have wilted.

5. Distribute the fried rice between two bowls, and top each bowl with half of the tofu.

6. Carefully wipe the pan out with paper towel again and spray with olive oil. Return to the heat and crack in the eggs. Cook to your liking – a minute or so for a runny yolk and sunny-side up, or flip over and cook for another minute for a well-cooked egg.

7. To serve, top each bowl of rice with a fried egg, a sprinkle of spring onion and the remaining coriander.

8. Serve with sliced cucumber and chilli, if you wish.

French-style Vegetable and Lentil Soup

Serves 2

SOUP

1 tablespoon olive oil

½ leek, white and light green parts only, finely sliced and washed

1 large carrot, quartered lengthways and roughly chopped

2 celery stalks, halved lengthways and roughly chopped

1 large zucchini, quartered lengthways and roughly chopped

1 garlic clove, minced

Sea salt and freshly ground black pepper

600 ml vegetable stock (or chicken stock or bone broth if you are not vegetarian)

1 x 400 g tin lentils, rinsed and drained

35 g (1 cup tightly packed) washed and roughly chopped silverbeet

2 tablespoons roughly chopped flat-leaf parsley

GARLIC CROSTINI

1 small wholegrain baguette

Extra-virgin olive oil

1 garlic clove, peeled

The beauty of this soup is that you can add any vegetables you have lying around, so it's a perfect way of using up the odds and ends from the fridge. It also happens to make for a warming, and filling, meal.

1. Heat a large saucepan or stockpot over medium heat. Add the olive oil, then add the leek, carrot, celery, zucchini, garlic and a good pinch of salt and pepper. Fry for 5–7 minutes, or until the vegetables have softened.

2. Add the stock, lentils and silverbeet and stir well. Bring to the boil, then turn the heat down and place the lid on the pan. Simmer for 10 minutes, or until the vegetables are cooked.

3. While the soup is cooking, prepare the garlic crostini. Preheat the oven grill to medium–high. Halve the baguette lengthways and toast it, uncut-side up, for a few minutes, or until beginning to turn golden.

4. Take the baguette out of the oven and drizzle a little extra-virgin olive oil over the cut sides. Add a good pinch of sea salt, then rub with the garlic clove and place back under the grill, cut-side up, to toast for a minute or so more.

5. Once the soup is ready, turn off the heat and stir in the parsley. Divide between two bowls and serve with the garlic crostini alongside.

5:2 option

Omit the walnuts and chickpea burger.

| PER SERVE | 240 CALORIES | 1003 KILOJOULES |

Vegan Grazing Platter

Serves 2

40 g (⅓ cup) walnuts

Olive oil spray

1 vegan chickpea burger

½ bunch baby carrots or 1 carrot, cut into large wedges

2 celery stalks, cut into large wedges

4 radishes, quartered

8 dill pickles (look for ones with no added sugar, such as polskie ogorkie)

4 pickled onions

10 olives

4 tablespoons store-bought vegan hummus

4 original Ryvitas

One of our favourite weekend lunches at home is a shared platter of any 'bits and bobs' we have floating around in the fridge and cupboard. I love eating this way because there's so much variety and each mouthful is a little different.

1. Toast the walnuts in a dry frying pan over medium–low heat for a few minutes, tossing occasionally. Keep an eye on them: once you can smell their nuttiness transfer immediately to a small bowl.

2. Spray the pan with olive oil and return it to the heat. Fry the chickpea burger for a few minutes on each side, or until cooked through, then quarter.

3. Arrange all of the ingredients attractively on a serving platter and share between two people.

Israeli Cauliflower 'Rice' with Felafels

Serves 2

½ head cauliflower, broken into florets

½ tablespoon olive oil

1 spring onion, finely sliced

60 g (½ cup) mushrooms, finely sliced

1 garlic clove, minced

Sea salt and freshly ground black pepper

½ teaspoon ground cumin

½ teaspoon ground coriander

2 tablespoons sultanas

Zest and juice of ½ lemon

50 g baby spinach leaves

¼ cup toasted nuts and seeds (a mixture of pepitas, sunflower seeds, flaked or slivered almonds, pine nuts or pistachios)

2 tablespoons roughly chopped coriander

2 tablespoons roughly chopped flat-leaf parsley

240 g (about 3 large or 6 small) good-quality store-bought felafels, cooked or heated according to the packet instructions

GARLIC YOGHURT SAUCE

130 g (½ cup) plain Greek-style yoghurt

½ garlic clove, minced

Juice of ½ lemon

I'm such a big fan of cauliflower. It's so rich in a wide variety of nutrients, such as vitamins C and K, folate and fibre, plus it's really versatile. It's a great lighter alternative to rice, not to mention a delicious way to up your serves of vegetables.

1. To make the yoghurt sauce, place all the ingredients into a small bowl. Add a good pinch of salt and stir together well. Place in the fridge until you're ready to serve.
2. Pulse the cauliflower florets in a food processor until they resemble grains of rice.
3. Place a large frying pan over medium heat. Add the olive oil, then add the spring onion and mushroom and cook for a few minutes or until they begin to soften.
4. Add the cauliflower 'rice' and the garlic to the pan with a good pinch of salt and pepper and continue to cook for another 2–3 minutes.
5. Add the ground spices, sultanas, lemon zest, juice and baby spinach to the pan. Stir to combine and cook until the spinach has wilted.
6. Turn the heat off and add the toasted seeds and nuts along with the chopped herbs and stir together well.
7. Divide between two bowls and top each serving with half of the felafel and a dollop of garlic yoghurt sauce.

Mediterranean Haloumi Salad

Serves 2

100 g (½ cup) pearl barley (see recipe introduction)

2 large zucchini, very thinly sliced lengthways (use a mandoline if you have one)

1 large eggplant, very thinly sliced lengthways (use a mandoline if you have one)

Olive oil spray

160 g (about 1 bunch) asparagus, trimmed

1 tablespoon olive oil

1 red onion, halved and thinly sliced

Sea salt and freshly ground black pepper

100 g haloumi

2 tablespoons roughly chopped mint + a little extra for the yoghurt dressing and for serving

100 g rocket leaves

1 tablespoon za'atar (see page 195)

A small handful of slivered almonds, toasted

YOGHURT AND SESAME DRESSING

2 tablespoons plain fat-free Greek-style yoghurt

1 teaspoon tahini

½ garlic clove, minced

Juice of 1 lemon

The Mediterranean diet is considered one of the best in the world because it's rich in plant foods, wholegrains, nuts, seeds and olive oil. This salad has all of those elements, plus some salty, squeaky goodness thanks to a little pan-fried haloumi. The pearl barley can be enjoyed warm or cold in the salad – both ways are lovely.

1. Preheat the oven grill to high. Cook the pearl barley according to the packet instructions. Set aside while you prepare the rest of the salad.

2. Place the zucchini and eggplant slices on a large baking tray and spray with olive oil – do this in a few batches if you need to. Cook under the grill for a few minutes on each side until golden and soft, but still holding their shape. Remove from the oven and set aside on a plate.

3. Heat a small frying pan over medium heat and add the asparagus spears. Cook for 4–5 minutes, shaking the pan every now and then, until they are cooked but still a little firm. Set aside on a plate.

4. Put the pan back over the heat and add half of the olive oil. Add the onion with a little pinch of salt and fry for 5 minutes or until softened, then set aside on a plate. Carefully wipe the pan out with paper towel.

5. Thinly slice the haloumi into 8 pieces. Place the frying pan back over the heat and add the remaining olive oil. Add the haloumi and fry for a minute or so on each side, or until golden.

6. Meanwhile, add all of the dressing ingredients to a small bowl with a pinch of chopped mint and season well with salt and pepper. It should be the consistency of a bottled creamy dressing – add a teaspoon of water or a little more, if needed, to reach your desired consistency.

7. Divide the mint and rocket between two plates. Top with the pearl barley, zucchini and eggplant slices and the pan-fried haloumi. Drizzle over the dressing and sprinkle over the za'atar, toasted almonds and some extra chopped mint.

5:2 option

Use only olive oil spray
instead of regular olive oil.
Omit the pearl barley and
the toasted almonds.

PER SERVE	330 CALORIES	1379 KILOJOULES

5:2 option

Use olive oil spray instead of regular olive oil and omit the couscous and the yoghurt dressing.

PER SERVE	275 CALORIES	1149 KILOJOULES

Warm Chickpea and Cauliflower Salad with Honey Roasted Carrots

Serves 2

8 baby carrots, tops trimmed

1½ tablespoons olive oil

1 teaspoon honey

Sea salt and freshly ground black pepper

½ head cauliflower, broken into florets or cut into wedges

½ teaspoon ground cumin

½ teaspoon ground coriander

1 leek, white and light green parts only, finely sliced and washed

1 garlic clove, minced

200 g (1 cup) drained and rinsed tinned chickpeas

300 g (2 cups) cooked couscous

100 g baby spinach leaves

2 tablespoons roughly chopped flat-leaf parsley

1 tablespoon sunflower seeds, toasted

YOGHURT DRESSING

130 g (½ cup) plain Greek-style yoghurt

Juice of ½ lemon

You won't ever miss meat with this delicious vegetarian dish! Soft, sweet carrots with spicy chickpeas and cauliflower is such a lovely mix, and this can be enjoyed as a warm dish or served cold as leftovers the next day.

1. To make the yoghurt dressing, place the yoghurt and lemon juice in a small bowl with a good pinch of sea salt. Stir together well, then place in the fridge until you're ready to serve.
2. Preheat the oven to 180°C. Line two baking trays with baking paper and arrange the carrots on one of them. Drizzle ½ tablespoon of the olive oil and the honey over the carrots, and season with salt and pepper.
3. Arrange the cauliflower on the other prepared tray. Drizzle ½ tablespoon of olive oil over the cauliflower, then season with salt and pepper and sprinkle over the ground spices. Place both trays of vegetables in the oven and cook for 20–30 minutes or until everything is golden and soft.
4. In the meantime, heat a large frying pan over medium heat and add the remaining olive oil. Add the leek, garlic and a pinch of salt, and fry gently for 4–5 minutes, or until the leek has softened.
5. Add the chickpeas and couscous to the pan and toss together for a minute to warm through. Turn off the heat and add the baby spinach and parsley. Toss everything together in the pan and allow the spinach to wilt.
6. To serve, divide the ingredients between two plates (or arrange on a large serving board). Sprinkle over the toasted sunflower seeds and drizzle with yoghurt dressing.

Four-bean Chilli with Mountain Bread Nachos

Serves 2

FOUR-BEAN CHILLI

1 tablespoon olive oil

½ onion, finely diced

Sea salt and freshly ground black pepper

1 eggplant, most of the skin trimmed off, flesh cut into 1 cm cubes

½ garlic clove, minced

1 x 400 g tin four-bean mix, drained and rinsed

1 teaspoon smoked paprika

½ teaspoon vegetable stock powder

1 heaped tablespoon tomato paste

1 x 400 g tin crushed tomatoes

2 Mountain Bread wraps (any flavour you wish)

GUACAMOLE

½ small avocado

Juice of ½ lime

TO SERVE

Grated cheese of your choice (if you're not vegan)

4 tablespoons chunky bottled salsa

Pickled jalapeños (optional)

Sour cream (use coconut yoghurt if you want to keep this recipe vegan)

Nachos can be rich, and quite a high-fat dish, but I've boosted this version by swapping meat for nutritionally rich beans, and making my own crispy Mountain Bread nachos in place of high-calorie chips.

1. To make the guacamole, put the avocado and lime juice in a small bowl with a good pinch of salt and roughly mash. Cover and place in the fridge until you're ready to serve.
2. Preheat the oven to 180°C. Line a baking tray with baking paper.
3. Heat a large non-stick frying pan over medium heat. Add the olive oil and onion and a pinch of salt and pepper. Cook for 5 minutes, or until the onion begins to soften.
4. Add the eggplant and continue to cook for a few more minutes, until soft.
5. Add the garlic, beans, paprika, stock powder, tomato paste and tinned tomatoes. Half-fill the empty tomato tin with water and add that to the pan as well. Bring to the boil, then turn down the heat to medium–low and partially cover with a lid. Simmer for 15 minutes, or until the mixture is thick and most of the water has evaporated.
6. Meanwhile, slice the wraps into 2 cm-thick strips. Lay these on the baking tray and bake for 5 minutes, or until golden. Take them out of the oven and leave on the tray for a couple of minutes to get crunchy.
7. Divide the chilli between two small bowls, arrange the 'nacho' chips around the edge and top with grated cheese, guacamole, chunky salsa, some pickled jalapeños and a dollop of sour cream.

Eggplant and Ricotta 'Cannelloni'

Serves 2

CANNELLONI

1 large eggplant

Olive oil spray

Sea salt and freshly ground black pepper

5 tablespoons basil leaves

280 g (1 cup) fresh low-fat ricotta

25 g (¼ cup) coarsely grated parmesan

250 ml (1 cup) tomato passata

30 g reduced-fat shredded mozzarella cheese

170 g (1 cup) polenta

GREEN SALAD

60 g (about ½ bag) of mixed salad leaves, such as rocket and baby spinach leaves

1 teaspoon extra-virgin olive oil

1 teaspoon red wine vinegar

Little rolls of eggplant make perfect soft 'cannelloni' in this dish. This can be enjoyed as a main meal served with polenta or as a side dish served with a protein of your choice.

1. Preheat the oven to 200°C. Line a large baking tray with baking paper.

2. Slice the eggplant lengthways into 8 slices about 0.5–1 cm thick. Spray each side with olive oil and lay the slices in a single layer on the trays. Sprinkle over a pinch of salt and pepper and bake for around 10 minutes, or until golden.

3. While the eggplant is cooking, prepare the ricotta filling. Roughly chop 4 tablespoons of the basil (reserving the rest for later) and place in a bowl with the ricotta and parmesan. Season well with salt and pepper and stir together.

4. Remove the eggplant from the oven. Once it has cooled enough to handle, start assembling the cannelloni. Place a tablespoon of the ricotta mixture towards the thicker end of one of the eggplant slices. Roll it up firmly, then place in a small baking dish, seam-side down. Repeat with the remaining eggplant slices and ricotta mixture and arrange so the rolls fit snugly together in the tray.

5. Pour the passata over the eggplant rolls so they are well covered. Scatter over the remaining basil leaves and sprinkle over the mozzarella cheese.

6. Bake for 10–15 minutes, or until the mozzarella is melted and golden.

7. While the cannelloni are baking, prepare the polenta according to the packet instructions.

8. Place the salad leaves in a bowl and drizzle with the extra-virgin olive oil and vinegar. Season with salt and pepper, then toss together well.

9. Serve 4 cannelloni per person with a spoonful of polenta and the green salad.

🌱 **5:2 option**

Omit the polenta.

PER SERVE	325 CALORIES	1358 KILOJOULES

Whole Roasted Cauliflower with Mushroom Sauce

Serves 2

ROASTED CAULIFLOWER

1 head cauliflower

1 tablespoon olive oil

Sea salt and freshly ground black pepper

MUSHROOM SAUCE

½ tablespoon olive oil

1 onion, finely sliced

240 g (2 cups) finely sliced button mushrooms

Splash of white wine

2 garlic cloves, minced

1 teaspoon fresh or dried thyme

3 tablespoons liquid chicken or vegetable stock

2 tablespoons plain, unsweetened coconut yoghurt

GARLIC SPINACH

½ tablespoon olive oil

1 garlic clove, minced

200 g baby spinach leaves, washed

Mashed potato, to serve

Cauliflower is the hero in this dish, and baking it whole is a wonderful way to enjoy it. It always amazes me that a humble, often overlooked vegetable like the cauliflower can emerge from the oven and be transformed into golden glory.

1. Preheat the oven to 200°C. Prepare the cauliflower by using a small knife to trim most of the leaves and stalk. Carefully cut out a little of the cauliflower's core, making sure you create a flat base. Sit the cauliflower in a deep baking dish. Drizzle over the olive oil and use your hands to massage it all over. Season generously with salt and pepper. Cover the dish tightly with foil and bake in the oven for 1 hour.

2. Remove the foil and bake for another 45–60 minutes, or until the cauliflower has turned a deep golden colour and is very tender.

3. Make the mashed potato while the cauliflower is cooking, then cover and set aside to keep warm.

4. Prepare the mushroom sauce about 15 minutes before you are ready to serve. Heat a medium non-stick frying pan over medium heat and add the olive oil, onion and mushroom and a good pinch of salt and pepper. Cook for 5–10 minutes, or until the mushrooms release their liquid and turn golden.

5. Deglaze the pan with a splash of white wine, scraping the base with a wooden spoon to pick up the lovely flavours. Cook for 2–3 minutes, then add the minced garlic, thyme, stock and coconut yoghurt. Bring to a simmer for a few minutes to thicken slightly.

6. To make the garlic spinach, heat a small frying pan over medium heat and add the olive oil. Fry the minced garlic gently for a minute, but don't let it brown. Add the spinach in batches as it wilts. It will seem like a lot of spinach but it will reduce down a lot in size. Turn the spinach gently in the pan until it has all wilted down.

7. Spoon the mashed potato onto the plates. Top with the spinach and the mushroom sauce, then place the roasted cauliflower on top.

Vegan Super Bowl

Serves 2

SUPER BOWL

200 g (1 cup) brown rice

150 g (1 cup) pumpkin,
cut into 1 cm cubes

Sea salt and freshly ground
black pepper

100 g cooked edamame
(see recipe introduction)

70 g (1 cup) finely shredded
red cabbage

1 carrot, coarsely grated or spiralised

160 g (1 cup) broccoli florets,
lightly steamed

½ small avocado, peeled and
finely diced

GREEN GODDESS DRESSING

½ small avocado

Juice of 1 lemon

1 spring onion, quartered

2 tablespoons fat-free plain
Greek-style yoghurt

2 tablespoons basil leaves

2 tablespoons parsley leaves

Super bowls, or 'buddha bowls', are very popular these days, and for good reason – they contain a wide variety of nutritious ingredients. I love including edamame (soy beans) in mine. You can buy packets of frozen edamame in most supermarkets. Either thaw them out before using, or blanch them in hot or boiling water for a minute or two.

1. Cook the brown rice according to the packet instructions.
2. Preheat the oven to 200°C. Line a baking tray with baking paper and spread the pumpkin onto the tray. Season with a pinch of salt and pepper, then dry bake for 15 minutes or until the pumpkin is soft and golden.
3. To make the dressing, add all the ingredients to a food processor and pulse until well combined.
4. Divide the ingredients for the super bowl between two shallow bowls, arranging them around the edge so you can see each of the ingredients.
5. Drizzle each bowl with half of the green goddess dressing before serving.

Fasting FAQs

I get a lot of questions about fasting at my clinic. Here are a few answers to some of the most common questions.

Q: I was told breakfast was the most important meal of the day but my part-day fasting routine means that I'm now skipping it. Is this okay?

A: The research is divided when it comes to whether we should eat breakfast or not and there are pros and cons to each argument. Some research has shown that regular breakfast eaters tend to be less heavy than breakfast skippers, however some people find they're more hungry and eat more over the day if they have breakfast. On the other hand, research has also shown that breakfast skippers (fasters) burn more fat when in fasting mode and are less hungry, and therefore eat less total calories over the day and have fewer food cravings if they fast in the morning.

Finding a middle ground such as having a late breakfast and an early dinner may be the best way to follow a fasting regime but at the end of the day, when and how you fast is very personal, and it needs to be sustainable for you and your lifestyle.

Q: Can I add milk to my tea or coffee if I'm fasting through the morning?

A: This depends on what you're trying to achieve with fasting. If weight loss is your goal then it's best to stick to black tea or coffee, which has no calories. If you just can't manage drinking your coffee without something, then you can add sweeteners like stevia or xylitol and just a dash (20–30 ml) of milk. The best milks to use 'strategically' for fasting are unsweetened almond or low-fat coconut milk because they contain little to no carbohydrates, which will help to prevent a rise in insulin and keep you in fasting mode. Otherwise simply use your choice of milk. The bottom line is that using a little milk in your drink to make it more palatable is better than no fasting at all.

If however, anti-ageing is your goal for fasting, it's recommended that you avoid all food or drinks completely with the exception for water because they disrupt the process of autophagy, which is triggered by fasting. This is the process of cleaning out damaged cells and regenerating new ones.

Q. I've been fasting for 2 months now, but I don't seem to be losing any weight. What's going on?

A. As with any weight and health journey, everybody responds to diet and lifestyle change differently – one regime might see someone dropping weight very quickly, while another person may not lose any weight. I think it's important to monitor yourself closely and make sure the regime you're doing is right for you. It might also be helpful to keep a food diary to reflect on what you're doing and make sure you're following your chosen fasting method properly.

Secondly, you may need to ramp up your fasting intensity, or perhaps your exercise intensity. Check your extras too – what's your alcohol intake? Are you treating yourself to foods like chips and chocolate more often than you realise?

I see a lot of patients in my clinic who weigh themselves at home then get into a state because they haven't lost any weight according to their scales. Although scales are a useful tool, they are ultimately not very helpful when trying to determine if you're experiencing fat loss, so taking measurements is key. I find the navel line, the widest part of your hips and along the nipple line are some of the best points to measure when tracking your progress. It's not uncommon for measurements to reduce nicely but for the weight on your scales to stay the same. You can also keep things simple and just use a pair of tight, unforgiving jeans to see how they fit.

At the end of the day, when and how you fast is very personal, and it needs to be sustainable for you and your lifestyle.

Q: Some days I only fast for 14 or 15 hours instead of my intended 16 hours. Will I still get the benefits of fasting?

A: The more regulated you can be with your fasting times, the better. That said, fasting for any length of time beyond 12 hours will have positive health and metabolic benefits, so don't worry too much if you sometimes fall short of the 16-hour fasting target.

Q: I've heard that some people have to stop fasting because their hormones go out of whack. Is there any truth to this?

A: There is anecdotal evidence that some women may not be suited to intermittent fasting because their hormones may be more sensitive to a change in their energy intake. For this reason, I suggest that if you are concerned about this and want to trial intermittent fasting, start with the very lightest option. This might mean limiting your eating window to 12 hours per day and then gently increasing the intensity to a 10-hour eating window and closely monitoring your mood and menstrual cycle.

Q: I often make it most of the way through a full-day fasting day, only to cave in right around dinner, overeating and blowing my calories for the day. How can I avoid this happening?

A: This is very typical dieting behaviour – restricting then blowing out. I'd really suggest avoiding full-day fasting if this happens to you regularly. If you can make it through a fasting day though, perhaps 16:8 fasting is better suited to you and worth trying.

Sometimes two full fasting days a week can be a bit hard going, so if you can manage just one day a week as well as some part-day fasting days, you will likely see similar benefits.

Fasting-friendly ingredients

PROTEINS

PORTION	CALORIES/ KJ PER SERVE
100 g chicken breast	**105 cals/950 kj**
100 g turkey breast	**120 cals/502 kj**
100 g pork medallion	**112 cals/468 kj**
100 g extra lean beef mince	**129 cals/539 kj**
2 eggs	**120 cals/502 kj**
100 g prawns (just flesh)	**89 cals/372 kj**
100 g squid	**78 cals/326 kj**
100 g plain white fish	**90 cals/376 kj**
95 g tin tuna in oil, drained	**113 cals/472 kj**
50 g smoked salmon (about 2 slices)	**105 cals/439 kj**

DAIRY & DAIRY SUBSTITUTES

PORTION	CALORIES/ KJ PER SERVE
250 ml (1 cup) skim milk	**90 cals/376 kj**
250 ml (1 cup) unsweetened almond milk (Almond Breeze)	**40 cals/167 kj**
250 ml (1 cup) unsweetened almond and coconut milk (So Good)	**43 cals/180 kj**
1 small tub fat-free, no sugar added Greek yoghurt (Chobani/ YoPro)	**100 cals/418 kj**
2 tablespoons reduced-fat ricotta or cottage cheese	**30 cals/125 kj**

VEGETARIAN & VEGAN PROTEIN SOURCES

PORTION	CALORIES/ KJ PER SERVE
100 g firm tofu	130 cals/543 kj
½ cup tinned lentils	75 cals/313 kj
½ cup tinned beans (borlotti, chickpea, black beans)	107 cals/447 kj
100 g silken tofu	65 cals/272 kj

VEGETABLES

PORTION	CALORIES/ KJ PER SERVE
100 g baby spinach leaves	20 cals/83 kj
1 cucumber	12 cals/49 kj
1 small carrot	32 cals/132 kj
1 cup shredded cabbage	15 cals/63 kj
10 snow peas	12 cals/50 kj
1 celery stalk	5 cals/19 kj
1 cup broccoli (broken into small florets)	50 cals/209 kj
1 cup sliced mushrooms	30 cals/124 kj

CARBOHYDRATES & STARCHES

PORTION	CALORIES/ KJ PER SERVE
1 slice wholegrain bread (50 g)	100 cals/418 kj
¼ cup raw rolled oats	115 cals/481 kj
2 high-fibre crackers (Vita-Weat)	45 cals/188 kj
1 Mountain Bread wrap	70 cals/293 kj

GREAT LOW-CALORIE 'FASTING FILLER FOODS'

PORTION	CALORIES/ KJ PER SERVE
125 g (drained weight) Slendier Noodles (½ of a 400 g packet)	13 cals/54 kj
113 g kelp noodles (⅓ of a 340 g packet)	6 cals/25 kj
1 cup cauliflower 'rice'	50 cals/209 kj
2 egg whites	30 cals/125 kj
Zucchini 'zoodles' (made from 1 medium zucchini)	35 cals/146 kj

FRUIT

PORTION	CALORIES/ KJ PER SERVE
125 g punnet blueberries or raspberries	65 cals/272 kj
250 g punnet strawberries	65 cals/272 kj
1 kiwi fruit	40 cals/167 kj
1 mandarin	40 cals/167 kj
1 small apple	50 cals/209 kj
1 orange	70 cals/293 kj
1 peach	50 cals/209 kj
1 small plum	30 cals/125 kj
1 small apricot	15 cals/63 kj
1 cup diced papaya	50 cals/209 kj
1 cup diced rockmelon	50 cals/209 kj
1 medium passionfruit	20 cals/84 kj
6 cherry tomatoes	20 cals/84 kj

FATS

PORTION	CALORIES/ KJ PER SERVE
1 spritz of olive oil spray	15 cals/63 kj
6 medium olives	20 cals/84 kj
10 pistachios	40 cals/167 kj

LOW (OR NO) CALORIE FLAVOURINGS & SAUCES

These fridge and pantry staples will add flavour and excitement to your meals without adding excess calories.

* Bone broths and bone broth powder

* Cinnamon – stick or ground

* Chilli flakes

* Chilli powder

* Chilli sauce

* Fish sauce

* Fresh and dried herbs (parsley, basil, coriander, mint, sage, oregano, thyme)

* Garlic – fresh, ground or minced

* Ginger – fresh, ground or minced

* Harissa paste

* Soy sauce

* Spices such as nutmeg, paprika, cumin, Chinese five spice, cayenne pepper

* Sriracha sauce

* Stevia leaf powder

* Stevia leaf concentrate

* Stock – liquid, powder or cubes (I like the Massel brand because it tastes great and includes vegan, gluten-free and low-FODMAP stocks that can be used by almost everyone!)

* Tomato sauce (with no added sugar)

* Tamari (looks and tastes like soy sauce but is wheat-free)

* Turmeric – fresh, ground or minced

* Vinegar (white, red, balsamic and rice wine vinegars – avoid sweet and sticky balsamic vinegar)

* Za'atar (a Middle Eastern spice mix available in some supermarkets and specialty grocers and markets)

Notes

Page 8 Research shows that a mere one in six …: J.L. Kraschnewski et al., 'Long-term weight loss maintenance in the United States', *International Journal of Obesity*, 2010, vol. 34. no.11, pp. 1644–1654

Page 8 Not only did fasting not cause the rats to become malnourished …: P. Sachdev, 'Fasting for a longer healthy life: Is there a scientific basis?', cheba.unsw.edu.au/blog/fasting-longer-healthy-life-there-scientific-basis

Page 8 About five years after watching that program I read a summary …: K.A. Varady et al., 'Effects of 8-hour time restricted feeding on body weight and metabolic disease risk factors in obese adults: A pilot study', *Nutrition and Healthy Aging*, 2018, vol. 4, no. 4, pp. 345–353. doi: 10.3233/NHA-170036

Page 24 According to Dr Michael Mosley, our body is preparing for sleep …: M. Mosley (Presenter), *Trust Me, I'm a Doctor* (Television Series), Episode 3, Series 7, 2018, London, UK: BBC TWO

Page 42 Research … shows that there is a transition period after three to six weeks …: V.D. Longo & M.P. Mattson, 'Fasting: Molecular Mechanisms and Clinical Applications', *Cell Metabolism*, 2014, vol. 19, no. 2, pp. 181–192. doi: 10.1016/j.cmet.2013.12.008

Page 46 However, studies show that intermittent fasting might increase endurance …: C. Paddock, 'How fasting boosts exercise's effects on endurance', medicalnewstoday.com/articles/321056.php

Page 60 But research suggests that eating for more than 15 hours of the day …: D. Zinczenko & P. Moore, *The 8-Hour Diet: Watch the Pounds Disappear Without Watching What You Eat*, 2015, New York, USA, St. Martin's Press

Page 60 Once those glycogen stores have been depleted …: S.M. Secor & H.V. Carey, 'Integrative Physiology of Fasting', *Comprehensive Physiology*, 2016, vol. 6, pp. 773–825. doi:10.1002/cphy.c150013

Page 60 Depending on your level of physical activity …: Longo & Mattson., 'Fasting: Molecular Mechanisms and Clinical Applications'

Page 62 Incredibly, in animal studies, intermittent fasting was shown …: Ibid

Page 62 Obesity is a major worldwide issue that is rapidly worsening …: European Associate for the Study of Obesity (EASO), 'Obesity Facts & Figures: Useful Resources from the WHO Regional Offices in Europe', 2013, easo.org/education-portal/obesity-facts-figures/

Page 62 Globally, at least 2.8 million people a year die from being overweight or obese …: Ibid

Page 62 3%: The average body weight lost in a study of overweight men and women …: K. Gabel et al., 'Time-restricted feeding (16:8) for weight loss in adults with obesity', *Nutrition and Healthy Aging*, 2018.

Page 63 Studies of people doing 5:2 or alternate-day fasting ...: S. Eshghinia & F. Mohammadzadeh., 'The effects of modified alternate-day fasting on weight loss and CAD risk factors in overweight and obese women', *Journal of Diabetes & Metabolic Disorders,* 2013. doi: 10.1186/2251-6581-12-4

Page 63 100 overweight people lost 6 per cent of their body weight ...: K.A. Varady et al., 'Alternate day fasting for weight loss in normal weight and overweight subjects: a randomized controlled trial', *Nutrition Journal,* 2013, vol. 12, no. 1. doi: 10.1186/1475-2891-12-146

Page 63 In one study, post-menopausal women lost twice as much weight ...: A. Barnosky et al., 'Effect of alternate day fasting on markers of bone metabolism: An exploratory analysis of a 6-month randomized controlled trial', *Journal of Nutritional Healthy Aging,* 2017, vol. 4, no. 3, pp. 255-263. doi: 10.3233/NHA-170031

Page 63 A group of young overweight women doing 5:2 ...: M. Harvie et al., 'The effects of intermittent or continuous energy restriction on weight loss and metabolic disease risk markers: a randomized trial in young overweight women', *International Journal of Obesity,* 2010, vol. 35, no. 5, pp. 714–727. doi: 10.1038/ijo.2010.171

Page 63 For people within a normal weight range, one study showed ...: K.A. Varady et al., 'Alternate day fasting for weight loss in normal weight and overweight subjects: a randomized controlled trial'

Page 63 On a traditional calorie-controlled diet ...: T. Moro et al., 'Effects of eight weeks of time-restricted feeding (16/8) on basal metabolism, maximal strength, body composition, inflammation and cardiovascular risk factors in resistance-trained males', *Journal of Translational Medicine,* 2016, vol. 14, p. 290. doi: 10.1186/s12967-016-1044-0

Page 63 Intermittent fasting maintains muscle mass ...: K.A. Varady et al, 'Alternate day fasting for weight loss in normal weight and overweight subjects: a randomized controlled trial'

Page 64 Cholesterol: Obese study participants following 16:8...: K. Gabel et al., 'Time-restricted feeding (16:8) for weight loss in adults with obesity'

Page 64 Cholesterol: A study of young men over two months ...: Moro et al, 'Effects of eight weeks of time-restricted feeding (16/8) on basal metabolism, maximal strength, body composition, inflammation and cardiovascular risk factors in resistance-trained males'

Page 64 Blood pressure: Obese men and women ...: Varady et al., 'Effects of 8-hour time restricted feeding on body weight and metabolic disease risk factors in obese adults: A pilot study'

Page 64 Cholesterol: A 12-month study on alternate-day fasting ...: Harvie et al., The effects of intermittent or continuous energy restriction on weight loss and metabolic disease risk markers: a randomized trial in young overweight women'

Page 64 Blood pressure: alternate-day and 5:2 fasting was shown to reduce blood pressure ...: Varady et al., 'Alternate day fasting for weight loss in normal weight and overweight subjects: a randomized controlled trial'

Page 67 Current research shows that intermittent fasting can yield incredible results ...: Moro et al., 'Effects of eight weeks of time-restricted feeding (16/8) on basal metabolism, maximal strength, body composition, inflammation and cardiovascular risk factors in resistance-trained males'
And also: K.A. Varady et. al., 'Alternate day fasting produces superior reductions versus daily calorie restriction in insulin resistance and other metabolic disease risk parameters in prediabetic adults' Submitted to *Nutrition Journal*, 2018

Page 67 Some scientists are going as far as saying that intermittent fasting can 'reverse' type 2 diabetes ...: A. Eenfeldt,. 'A book that should change the world: The Diabetes Code, by Dr. Jason Fung', 2018, dietdoctor.com/book-change-world-diabetes-code-dr-jason-fung

Page 67 Preliminary findings show part-day fasting has similar results to full-day fasting ...: Moro et al., 'Effects of eight weeks of time-restricted feeding (16/8) on basal metabolism, maximal strength, body composition, inflammation and cardiovascular risk factors in resistance-trained males'

Page 67 Young men who followed 16:8 for two months ...: Ibid

Page 67 The most significant results were seen in individuals with prediabetes ...: Varady et. al., 'Alternate day fasting produces superior reductions versus daily calorie restriction in insulin resistance and other metabolic disease risk parameters in prediabetic adults'

Page 67 Another study showed a 20–25 per cent reduction in insulin resistance ..: Harvie et al., 'The effects of intermittent or continuous energy restriction on weight loss and metabolic disease risk markers: a randomized trial in young overweight women'

Page 67 ... and up to 45 per cent in another study on people with prediabetes ...: Varady et. al., 'Alternate day fasting produces superior reductions versus daily calorie restriction in insulin resistance and other metabolic disease risk parameters in prediabetic adults'

Page 67 20%: The reduction in insulin levels in a study tracking non-diabetic obese adults ...: Harvie et al., 'The effects of intermittent or continuous energy restriction on weight loss and metabolic disease risk markers: a randomized trial in young overweight women'. And also: J.F. Trepanowski et al., 'Short-term modified alternate-day fasting: a novel dietary strategy for weight loss and cardioprotection in obese adults', 2017, gwern.net/docs/longevity/2017-trepanowski.pdf

Page 68 Fasting can reduce the recurrence of breast cancer in women ...: C.R. Marinac et al., 'Prolonged Nightly Fasting and Breast Cancer Prognosis' *JAMA Oncology*, 2016, vol. 2, no. 8, pp. 1049–1055. doi: 10.1001/jamaoncol.2016.0164

Page 68 Fasting can slow the growth of tumours ...: M.P. Cleary & M.E. Grossmann, 'The manner in which calories are restricted impacts mammary tumor cancer prevention', *Journal of Carcinogenesis*, 2011, vol. 10,no. 21. doi: 10.4103/1477-3163.85181

Page 68 Fasting can induce autophagy ...: E. White et. al., 'Autophagy, Metabolism and Cancer', *Clinical Cancer Research*, 2015, vol. 21, no. 22, clincancerres.aacrjournals.org/content/21/22/5037.long

Page 68 In animals, fasting can reduce ...: C. Lee & V.D. Longo, 'In animals, fasting can reduce insulin-like growth factor', *Oncogene*, 2011, issue 30, pp. 3305–3316, nature.com/articles/onc201191

Page 70 These new neurons and neuronal connections have also been shown …: W. Duan et. al., 'Brain-derived neurotrophic factor mediates an excitoprotective effect of dietary restriction in mice', *Journal of Neurochemistry*, 2001, Issue 76, pp. 619–626, doi: 10.1046/j.1471-4159.2001.00071.x

Page 70 Fasting can also help to improve mental clarity and focus …: M.P. Mattson et al., 'Impact of intermittent fasting on health and disease processes', *Aging Research Reviews*, 2016, vol. 39, pp. 46–58, doi: 10.1016/j.arr.2016.10.005

Page 70 This is believed to be due to the release of a hormone called catecholamine …: Future Health: The UWA Health Blog for Undergraduate Articles, 'Research-based health benefits of intermittent fasting', 2018, blogs.uwa.edu.au/futurehealth/2018/01/05/research-based-health-benefits-of-intermittent-fasting/

Page 70 Full-day 5:2 fasting has been shown to support brain health by improving memory …: Mattson et al., 'Impact of intermittent fasting on health and disease processes'

Page 71 Researchers have found that intermittent fasting produces a compound …: Y. Youm et al., 'The ketone metabolite β-hydroxybutyrate blocks NLRP3 inflammasome–mediated inflammatory disease', *Nature Medicine*, 2015, issue 21, pp. 263–269, nature.com/articles/nm.3804

Page 71 Studies have shown that fasting not only has the potential to restore normal gut microbiota …: Z.H. Rong et al.,'Effect of intermittent fasting on physiology and gut microbiota in presenium rats', *Journal of Southern Medical University*, 2016, vol. 37, issue 4, pp. 423–430, ncbi.nlm.nih.gov/pubmed/28446391

Page 74 Researchers are finding that the combination of exercise and intermittent fasting can slow ageing …: Longo & Mattson, 'Fasting: Molecular Mechanisms and Clinical Applications'

Page 74 Fasting is believed to promote healthy ageing by reducing certain biochemical markers …: Ibid

Page 74 In an animal study, rats that fasted for 24 hours …: Ibid

Page 188 If, however, anti-ageing is your goal for fasting …: A. Palanisamy, 'Is Coffee OK During Intermittent Fasting?', doctorakil.com/coffee-intermittent-fasting/

Page 190 There is anecdotal evidence that some women may not be suited …: H. Kollias, 'Intermittent Fasting for women: Important information you need to know'

Thank you ...

This book is a dream come true and something I've been wanting to write for so many years, so the very first person I need to thank is my publisher extraordinaire, Ingrid Ohlsson, for believing in me enough to give me the opportunity of a lifetime.

As a first-time author, the process of creating this book was completely new to me but was made so easy with support and guidance from the incredible Pan Macmillan team that included Virginia Birch, Megan Pigott and Naomi van Groll.

The words in this book are my experiences and knowledge from years of clinical practice and a whole lot of research, transported from my brain and onto paper. However, they'd be a big old mess if it wasn't for my amazing editor, Katie Bosher, who held my hand through changes and adjustments and explained to me what things like endnotes and first pages were. Also a big thank you to the very clever designers at Northwood Green who took my words, pictures and recipes and put it all together to create the most beautiful looking book.

It was my greatest delight watching my favourite recipes be brought to life by my foodie dream team of photographer Cath Muscat, food stylist Michelle Noerianto and chef Cynthia Black. I never in a million years could have imagined the recipes I created out of my kitchen at home could look so delicious and so beautiful.

A few personal thank yous I must add: To my mumma, Kerryn Phelps, thank you for paving the way for me by showing me what's possible for me and for my career outside of my day-to-day job, for always going where it's a little scary and almost always coming out on top. You are a daily inspiration. To my dad and my stepmum, who allowed me to go along with them on their health journeys – you helped me learn so much along the way. To my amazing hubby, you're my number-one fan and you have always had unwavering belief in me – you knew I could do this and more long before I did. And finally, to my baby boy, Billy. It's all for you. (I'm sobbing as I write this.) I hope with all my heart that I can inspire even just a few people with this book. If I can do that and make you a little bit proud, then my job is done.

CONVERSION CHART

Measuring cups and spoons may vary slightly from one country to another, but the difference is generally not enough to affect a recipe. All cup and spoon measures are level.

One Australian metric measuring cup holds 250 ml (8 fl oz), one Australian tablespoon holds 20 ml (4 teaspoons) and one Australian metric teaspoon holds 5 ml. North America, New Zealand and the UK use a 15 ml (3-teaspoon) tablespoon.

LENGTH

METRIC	IMPERIAL
3 mm	⅛ inch
6 mm	¼ inch
1 cm	½ inch
2.5 cm	1 inch
5 cm	2 inches
18 cm	7 inches
20 cm	8 inches
23 cm	9 inches
25 cm	10 inches
30 cm	12 inches

LIQUID MEASURES

ONE AMERICAN PINT	ONE IMPERIAL PINT
500 ml (16 fl oz)	600 ml (20 fl oz)

CUP	METRIC	IMPERIAL
⅛ cup	30 ml	1 fl oz
¼ cup	60 ml	2 fl oz
⅓ cup	80 ml	2½ fl oz
½ cup	125 ml	4 fl oz
⅔ cup	160 ml	5 fl oz
¾ cup	180 ml	6 fl oz
1 cup	250 ml	8 fl oz
2 cups	500 ml	16 fl oz
2¼ cups	560 ml	20 fl oz
4 cups	1 litre	32 fl oz

DRY MEASURES

The most accurate way to measure dry ingredients is to weigh them. However, if using a cup, add the ingredient loosely to the cup and level with a knife; don't compact the ingredient unless the recipe requests 'firmly packed'.

METRIC	IMPERIAL
15 g	½ oz
30 g	1 oz
60 g	2 oz
125 g	4 oz (¼ lb)
185 g	6 oz
250 g	8 oz (½ lb)
375 g	12 oz (¾ lb)
500 g	16 oz (1 lb)
1 kg	16 oz (1 lb)

OVEN TEMPERATURES

CELSIUS	FAHRENHEIT
100°C	200°F
120°C	250°F
150°C	300°F
160°C	325°F
180°C	350°F
200°C	400°F
220°C	425°F

CELSIUS	GAS MARK
110°C	¼
130°C	½
140°C	1
150°C	2
170°C	3
180°C	4
190°C	5
200°C	6
220°C	7
230°C	8
240°C	9
250°C	10

Index

First published 2019 in Macmillan
by Pan Macmillan Australia Pty Limited
1 Market Street, Sydney, New South Wales
Australia 2000

A CIP catalogue record for this book is available from the National Library
of Australia: catalogue.nla.gov.au

Design by Northwood Green
Photography by Cath Muscat
Prop and food styling by Michelle Noerianto
Food preparation by Cynthia Black
Editing by Katie Bosher
Makeup by Gloria Tulemija
Colour + reproduction by Splitting Image Colour Studio
Printed in China by 1010 Printing International Limited

10 9 8 7 6 5 4